The Ultimate Guide to Producing Different Kinds of Beer: A Beer Drinker's Handbook

Copyright Page

TITLE: The Ultimate Guide to Producing Different Kinds of Beer: A Beer Drinker's Handbook

1ST Edition

ISBN: 9798223987550

Table of Contents

The Ultimate Guide to Producing Different Kinds of Beer: A Beer Drinker's Handbook

By Roberto Miguel Rodriguez

Chapter 1: Introduction to Beer Production

The History and Evolution of Beer

Beer, one of the oldest and most beloved alcoholic beverages, has a rich and fascinating history that spans thousands of years. From its humble beginnings in ancient Mesopotamia to the craft beer revolution of the present day, beer has evolved and adapted to suit the tastes and preferences of beer drinkers across the globe.

The story of beer begins around 7,000 to 8,000 years ago in what is now modern-day Iraq. The Sumerians, an ancient civilization, were the first to cultivate barley and ferment it into beer. They even had a goddess of beer, Ninkasi, who was the patroness of brewing and the keeper of the secrets of fermentation.

As beer spread throughout the world, each culture put its own unique spin on the brewing process. In ancient Egypt, beer was a staple of daily life and was even used as currency. The Egyptians brewed a beer called "zythum" which was thick and often flavored with dates or honey.

In medieval Europe, monasteries played a crucial role in preserving and advancing the art of brewing. Monks brewed beer not only for sustenance but also as a means of financial support. They developed brewing techniques that are still used today, such as the use of hops as a natural preservative.

The Industrial Revolution in the 18th century brought significant changes to the beer industry. The invention of the steam engine and advances in technology allowed for mass production and distribution of beer. This led to the rise of large-scale commercial breweries and the standardization of beer styles.

However, in recent years, there has been a resurgence of interest in craft beer and home brewing. Beer drinkers are seeking out unique and innovative flavors, leading to the rise of small, independent breweries. Craft beer production techniques focus on quality ingredients, experimentation, and creativity, resulting in a wide range of beer styles and flavors.

Additionally, the demand for specialized beers has increased. Gluten-free beer production has become popular among those with gluten sensitivities, while barrel-aged beers and fruit-infused beers offer complex and exciting flavor profiles.

The history and evolution of beer have come full circle, with modern brewers exploring traditional brewing methods from around the world. Sour beers, which were once considered old-fashioned, have experienced a revival, with brewers using ancient fermentation techniques to create complex and tart flavors.

Whether it's brewing seasonal or holiday beers, pairing beer with food, or learning the basics of home brewing, beer drinkers today have a wealth of knowledge and resources at their disposal. The Ultimate Guide to Producing Different Kinds of Beer is a comprehensive handbook that covers all aspects of beer production, from traditional methods to the latest trends in craft brewing. So grab a pint, dive into the history and evolution of beer, and join the ever-growing community of beer enthusiasts around the world.

The Science Behind Brewing

Beer is not just a beverage; it is an art form that has been perfected over centuries. Behind every pint of delicious beer lies the intricate science of brewing. Understanding the scientific processes involved in brewing can elevate your appreciation for this beloved drink. In this subchapter, we delve into the science behind brewing, unraveling the secrets that make beer production a fascinating blend of chemistry and biology.

One of the key scientific aspects of brewing is fermentation. This process is responsible for transforming the sweet wort into the flavorful and intoxicating beer we all enjoy. Yeast, a single-celled organism, plays a vital role in fermentation. It consumes the sugars present in the wort and produces alcohol and carbon dioxide as byproducts. The temperature and type of yeast used greatly influence the flavor profile of the final product. We explore the different types of yeast and their impact on beer production, giving you the tools to experiment and create unique brews.

The quality of water used in brewing also plays a crucial role. Understanding the mineral content and pH of water can help brewers achieve desired flavors and characteristics in their beer. We discuss the importance of water chemistry and provide insights on how to adjust water to match specific beer styles.

Another scientific aspect of brewing is the mashing process, where enzymes break down complex carbohydrates into fermentable sugars. This process involves precise temperature control and enzymatic reactions that convert starches into sugars accessible to yeast. We delve into the science behind mashing and provide techniques to achieve optimal results.

Additionally, this subchapter explores the science behind carbonation, hop utilization, and how different brewing techniques influence beer flavors. We also touch on the scientific advancements that have revolutionized the craft beer industry, such as barrel aging, fruit infusion, and gluten-free beer production.

By understanding the science behind brewing, you can elevate your home brewing techniques or appreciate the craft beer you enjoy at your favorite brewery. Whether you are a beginner or a seasoned brewer, this subchapter provides valuable insights into the scientific processes that ultimately result in the perfect pint. So grab a beer, dive into the science behind brewing, and unlock the secrets to producing exceptional beer at home or appreciating the craft behind your favorite brews. Cheers!

Understanding Beer Styles

Beer is one of the oldest and most beloved alcoholic beverages in the world. With countless varieties and flavors, it can be overwhelming to choose the perfect beer for your taste. This subchapter aims to provide beer drinkers with a comprehensive understanding of different beer styles, allowing them to explore and appreciate the wide array of options available.

To begin, it is important to note that beer styles are not simply random classifications but rather a reflection of the ingredients, brewing techniques, and regional traditions. Each beer style has specific characteristics that make it unique and appealing to different palates.

The subchapter starts by delving into the basics of beer styles, discussing the main categories such as lagers, ales, stouts, and wheat beers. It further explores the subcategories within each style, providing a detailed description of their characteristics, ingredients, and brewing methods. Whether you prefer a crisp and refreshing lager, a full-bodied stout, or a fruity wheat beer, understanding the different styles will help you make an informed choice.

The subchapter also introduces the concept of craft beer production techniques, which have gained immense popularity in recent years. Craft beer enthusiasts will learn about the innovative methods employed by breweries to create unique and flavorful beers, such as dry hopping, barrel aging, and fruit infusion. Furthermore, it explores the growing trend of gluten-free beer production, catering to those with dietary restrictions.

For aspiring home brewers, this subchapter offers valuable insights into brewing sour beers, traditional brewing methods from around the world, and low-alcohol or non-alcoholic beer production. It provides step-by-step instructions and tips for beginners to successfully produce these specialized beers in the comfort of their own homes.

Lastly, the subchapter highlights the art of beer pairing and offers a selection of food recipes that complement various beer styles. From classic pairings like beer and cheese to more adventurous combinations, beer drinkers will discover the joys of enhancing their tasting experience through culinary exploration.

In conclusion, "Understanding Beer Styles" serves as an indispensable guide for beer drinkers, providing a wealth of knowledge about the vast world of beer. Whether you are a seasoned connoisseur or a novice enthusiast, this subchapter will enable you to appreciate the nuances of different beer styles and make informed choices based on your preferences. Cheers!

Chapter 2: How to Produce Different Kinds of Beer

The Basics of Beer Brewing

Beer, the beloved beverage enjoyed by millions around the world, is not just a drink to be savored but an art form to be appreciated. For those who have always wondered how this golden elixir is made, this subchapter titled "The Basics of Beer Brewing" will serve as your ultimate guide to understanding the process behind creating different kinds of beer.

Whether you are a beer enthusiast, an aspiring craft brewer, or a curious homebrewer, this chapter will provide you with the fundamental knowledge and techniques needed to produce your own unique brews. From traditional brewing methods from around the world to modern craft beer production techniques, we will explore it all.

We will start by delving into the ingredients that make up beer. From malted grains, hops, yeast, and water, each component plays a crucial role in the flavor, aroma, and appearance of the final product. You will learn how to select the right ingredients and understand their impact on the brewing process.

Next, we will guide you through the step-by-step process of brewing beer. From mashing and boiling to fermentation and bottling, we will explain each stage in detail, ensuring that you have a comprehensive understanding of the entire brewing process. You will also learn about the different equipment and tools needed for home brewing, making it accessible for beginners.

Once you have mastered the basics, we will delve into the exciting world of producing different kinds of beer. From sour beers to gluten-free and low-alcohol options, we will explore the techniques and ingredients required to create each unique style. We will also provide tips on how to infuse fruits into your beer for a refreshing twist.

To further expand your knowledge, we will introduce you to barrel-aged beer production, a process that imparts distinct flavors and complexities to the brew. Additionally, we will explore the art of brewing seasonal or holiday beers, perfect for those special occasions.

Lastly, we will touch upon beer pairing and food recipes, offering guidance on how to enhance your beer-drinking experience by matching it with delectable dishes. From cheese and charcuterie boards to hearty stews and desserts, you will discover the perfect culinary companions for your favorite beers.

Whether you are a novice homebrewer or an experienced craft beer connoisseur, "The Basics of Beer Brewing" will equip you with the knowledge and skills needed to produce a wide range of beer styles. So grab a pint, sit back, and let us take you on an exciting journey through the world of beer brewing. Cheers!

Brewing Equipment and Ingredients

When it comes to producing different kinds of beer, the right brewing equipment and top-quality ingredients are crucial. Whether you are a craft beer enthusiast or a home brewing beginner, understanding the equipment and ingredients required for the brewing process is essential. In this subchapter, we will delve into the world of brewing equipment and ingredients, providing you with the knowledge you need to create your own delicious beers.

To begin, let's talk about the equipment necessary for brewing beer. The most basic brewing setup consists of a brew kettle, fermentation vessel, airlock, and a hydrometer. However, as you delve deeper into the world of brewing, you may find it beneficial to invest in additional equipment such as a mash tun, wort chiller, and a kegging system. These tools will help you take your brewing skills to the next level, allowing you to experiment with various brewing techniques and produce professional-quality beers.

Next, let's move on to the key ingredients in beer production. The primary ingredients are water, malted grains, hops, and yeast. Water acts as the foundation of beer, and its quality and mineral content can greatly affect the final product. Malted grains, such as barley, provide the sugars necessary for fermentation. Hops add bitterness, aroma, and flavor to the beer, balancing out the sweetness of the malt. Yeast is responsible for fermentation, converting sugars into alcohol and carbon dioxide.

When it comes to producing different kinds of beer, the choice of ingredients becomes even more important. Craft beer production techniques often involve experimenting with unique malt and hop combinations to create distinct flavors and aromas. Home brewing beginners can start with simple recipes and gradually explore more complex ingredients and techniques. For those interested in brewing sour beers, specific strains of bacteria and yeast are used to achieve the desired tartness. Traditional brewing methods from around the world offer a glimpse into the rich history of beer production, with each region showcasing unique ingredients and brewing techniques.

For those with dietary restrictions, gluten-free beer production offers a solution. By using alternative grains, such as rice or sorghum, gluten-free beers can be brewed without sacrificing taste and quality. Barrel-aged beer production involves aging beer in wooden barrels, imparting unique flavors and characteristics. Fruit-infused beer brewing allows for endless possibilities, as various fruits can be added during fermentation to create vibrant and refreshing beers.

Whether you are interested in brewing low-alcohol or non-alcoholic beers, brewing seasonal or holiday beers, or exploring beer pairing and food recipes, understanding the right equipment and ingredients is vital. By mastering the art of brewing equipment and ingredients, you can unlock a world of creativity and flavor, producing a wide range of delicious beers to satisfy your palate and impress your friends.

Step-by-Step Brewing Process

Whether you're a craft beer enthusiast, a homebrewing beginner, or simply someone curious about the art of beer production, understanding the step-by-step brewing process is crucial. In this subchapter, we will walk you through the various stages involved in creating the perfect beer, showcasing the techniques used by professionals and seasoned homebrewers around the world.

1. Mashing and Malting: The brewing process begins with the careful selection of malted grains, such as barley, which are then crushed and mixed with hot water in a process called mashing. This step activates enzymes that convert starches into fermentable sugars.

2. Lautering and Sparging: Once the mashing is complete, the liquid mixture, known as wort, is separated from the spent grain through a process called lautering. This involves transferring the wort to a separate vessel while rinsing the grain bed with hot water in a process known as sparging.

3. Boiling and Hops Addition: The wort is then transferred to a brewing kettle, where it is brought to a rolling boil. During this stage, hops are added at different times to impart bitterness, flavor, and aroma to the beer. The length of the boil and the timing of hop additions greatly influence the final beer's characteristics.

4. Fermentation: After the boiling process, the wort is rapidly cooled and transferred to a fermentation vessel. Yeast is added, which

consumes the sugars in the wort and converts them into alcohol and carbon dioxide. This process typically takes one to two weeks, depending on the style of beer being brewed.

5. Conditioning and Carbonation: Once fermentation is complete, the beer is conditioned to allow any remaining yeast and sediment to settle. This can be done in a secondary fermentation vessel or directly in the serving keg or bottle. Carbonation can be achieved naturally through the fermentation process or by adding priming sugar before bottling.

6. Packaging and Storage: Finally, the beer is ready for packaging. Whether in bottles, cans, or kegs, proper sanitation is crucial to maintain the beer's quality. The beer is then stored in a cool, dark place for a period of time to allow flavors to harmonize and mature.

Understanding the step-by-step brewing process is not only fascinating but also empowers beer drinkers to appreciate the craftsmanship behind their favorite beverages. Whether you're interested in producing different kinds of beer, experimenting with craft beer production techniques, or even trying your hand at homebrewing, this guide serves as a comprehensive resource to help you master the art of brewing. So, grab a pint and dive into the world of beer production!

Common Issues and Troubleshooting

Beer production can be a complex process, and even experienced brewers can come across common issues that can affect the quality and taste of their brews. In this subchapter, we will explore some of the most common problems encountered during beer production and provide troubleshooting tips to help you overcome them.

One of the most frequent issues brewers face is fermentation problems. If your beer fails to ferment properly, it can result in off-flavors or a lack of carbonation. To troubleshoot this, ensure that you have the correct yeast strain for your beer style and that your fermentation temperature is within the recommended range. Additionally, make sure you have enough healthy yeast cells by properly pitching your yeast and aerating your wort.

Another issue that can arise is infection. Contamination from unwanted bacteria or wild yeast can ruin your beer. To prevent this, always sanitize your equipment thoroughly and maintain proper hygiene throughout the brewing process. If you suspect an infection, look for signs such as off-flavors, unusual smells, or a pellicle forming on the surface of your beer. In such cases, consider discarding the batch to avoid ruining future brews.

Carbonation problems can also occur. If your beer is under-carbonated, it may be due to insufficient priming sugar or a lack of fermentation activity. To fix this issue, you can try adding a small amount of priming sugar directly to each bottle before sealing them. If your beer is over-carbonated and prone to foaming, you may have used too much priming sugar. In this case, carefully release some pressure from the bottles to prevent them from exploding.

Lastly, clarity issues can affect the appearance of your beer. Hazy or cloudy beer can be caused by various factors such as incomplete fermentation, improper chilling, or inadequate fining. To improve clarity, ensure proper fermentation and cooling, and consider using fining agents such as Irish moss or gelatin during the brewing process.

By addressing these common issues and following the troubleshooting tips provided, you can enhance the quality of your homemade beer and avoid disappointment. Remember to experiment, learn from your mistakes, and enjoy the journey of producing different kinds of beer. Cheers to your brewing success!

Fermentation and Conditioning

Fermentation and Conditioning: The Heart and Soul of Beer Production

In the world of beer, fermentation and conditioning are the crucial steps that transform simple ingredients into the refreshing and flavorful beverages we all love. Understanding these processes is essential for anyone interested in producing different kinds of beer. Whether you are a craft beer enthusiast, a home brewer, or simply curious about traditional brewing methods from around the world, this subchapter will provide you with invaluable insights.

Fermentation is the magical transformation that occurs when yeast consumes the sugars present in the wort, creating alcohol and carbon dioxide. This is where the real art of brewing takes place. Different strains of yeast can dramatically impact the final flavor and aroma of the beer, allowing brewers to craft a wide variety of styles. From lagers to ales and everything in between, the fermentation process plays a crucial role in shaping the character of each beer.

Once the primary fermentation is complete, conditioning comes into play. This is a period of rest where the beer matures and develops its full potential. During this stage, flavors mellow, and any remaining yeast and sediment settle at the bottom of the vessel. Conditioning can take anywhere from a few days to several months, depending on the style and desired characteristics of the beer.

Craft beer production techniques often involve experimenting with fermentation and conditioning to create unique and innovative flavors. For example, brewing sour beers requires special attention to the fermentation process, as specific strains of bacteria are introduced to create the desired tartness. Similarly, barrel-aged beer production involves extended conditioning in wooden barrels, which imparts distinctive flavors and aromas.

Home brewers, especially those new to the craft, can benefit from understanding the importance of fermentation and conditioning. By carefully controlling temperature, yeast selection, and conditioning time, they can achieve professional-quality results in their own kitchens.

Traditional brewing methods from around the world also highlight the significance of fermentation and conditioning. From Belgian farmhouse ales to German lagers, each culture has its own unique approach to these processes, resulting in a rich tapestry of beer styles and flavors.

For those with specific dietary needs or preferences, such as gluten-free diets, understanding fermentation and conditioning can be the key to producing delicious alternatives. By utilizing gluten-free grains and carefully managing the fermentation and conditioning stages, brewers can create flavorful gluten-free beers that rival their traditional counterparts.

Whether you're interested in brewing fruit-infused beers, low-alcohol or non-alcoholic options, or seasonal and holiday brews, fermentation and conditioning are at the core of these endeavors. By mastering these techniques, beer enthusiasts can create perfectly balanced and well-rounded beverages that pair beautifully with a variety of foods.

In conclusion, fermentation and conditioning are the heart and soul of beer production. They are the steps that turn ordinary ingredients into extraordinary brews. By delving into these processes, beer drinkers can unlock a world of flavors and techniques that will enhance their appreciation of the craft and their ability to produce different kinds of beer. So raise a glass and cheers to the transformative power of fermentation and conditioning!

Packaging and Storage

When it comes to producing beer, the packaging and storage process is just as crucial as the brewing itself. Proper packaging and storage techniques ensure that the beer you produce maintains its quality, flavor, and freshness. In this subchapter, we will explore the various methods and best practices for packaging and storing different kinds of beer.

One of the most common packaging methods for beer is bottling. Whether you are a homebrewer or a craft brewery, bottling provides a convenient way to package your beer. It is important to use clean and sanitized bottles to prevent any contamination. You can either use traditional glass bottles or opt for more eco-friendly options like aluminum cans or PET bottles.

Another popular packaging method is kegging, which is commonly used by bars, restaurants, and microbreweries. Kegs offer a more efficient way to package large quantities of beer and are perfect for draft systems. Just like bottles, kegs should be properly cleaned and sanitized before filling them with beer.

Once your beer is packaged, it is crucial to store it correctly to maintain its quality. The ideal storage conditions include a cool and dark environment. Temperature fluctuations and exposure to light can negatively impact the flavor and aroma of beer. If you have limited storage space, consider investing in a temperature-controlled refrigerator or cellar.

For craft breweries and homebrewers, it is important to consider the shelf life of your beer. While some beer styles are meant to be consumed fresh, others can age and develop complex flavors over time. It is essential to research and understand the optimal aging period for each beer style you produce.

If you are producing fruit-infused or barrel-aged beers, the storage process becomes even more critical. These beers often require longer aging periods to develop their unique characteristics. Make sure to monitor the aging process closely and regularly sample the beer to ensure it is reaching its desired flavor profile.

Proper packaging and storage techniques are also essential for maintaining the quality of gluten-free, low-alcohol, or non-alcoholic beers. These specialized beers require additional care to preserve their unique qualities.

In conclusion, packaging and storage play a vital role in producing different kinds of beer. Whether you are a homebrewer or a craft brewery, understanding the best practices for packaging and storing beer is essential for maintaining its quality, flavor, and freshness. By following these guidelines, you can ensure that the beer you produce delights your taste buds every time you crack open a bottle or pour from a keg.

Chapter 3: Craft Beer Production Techniques

Small-Scale Craft Brewing

Craft brewing has gained immense popularity in recent years, with beer enthusiasts exploring unique flavors and experimenting with different brewing techniques. Small-scale craft brewing has become a thriving industry, offering beer drinkers a diverse range of flavors and styles to choose from. In this subchapter, we will delve into the world of small-scale craft brewing and uncover the secrets behind producing exceptional beers.

Craft beer production techniques play a crucial role in the creation of unique and flavorful brews. From selecting the finest ingredients to carefully controlling fermentation temperatures, every step in the brewing process contributes to the final product. Home brewing for beginners is a great way to enter the world of craft brewing, allowing beer lovers to experiment with different flavors and styles right from the comfort of their homes.

For those looking to push the boundaries of traditional brewing, sour beers offer a fascinating avenue to explore. Brewing sour beers requires patience and a keen understanding of the complex fermentation process. We will dive into the techniques and ingredients needed to create these tangy, mouth-puckering delights.

Traditional brewing methods from around the world provide a glimpse into the rich history of beer production. From Belgian farmhouse ales to German lagers, each brewing tradition has its own unique characteristics and brewing techniques. By exploring these traditional methods, beer drinkers can gain a deeper appreciation for the art of brewing.

The demand for gluten-free beer has been on the rise, and we will explore the techniques and ingredients used in gluten-free beer production. Barrel-aged beer production offers another exciting avenue for craft brewers, as the flavors imparted by wooden barrels add complexity and depth to the final brew.

Fruit-infused beer brewing is a popular technique among craft brewers, allowing them to add a burst of fruity flavors to their creations. We will explore the various fruits and methods used to infuse beer with these delightful flavors. Low-alcohol or non-alcoholic beer production has also gained traction, catering to those who prefer a milder brew without compromising on taste.

Seasonal or holiday beers provide a festive twist to traditional brewing. We will uncover the secrets behind brewing these limited-edition delights that capture the essence of different seasons and celebrations. Lastly, we will delve into the world of beer pairing and provide a collection of food recipes that perfectly complement the flavors of different beers, elevating the overall dining experience.

Whether you are a seasoned beer drinker or a homebrewing novice, this subchapter will equip you with the knowledge and techniques to produce different kinds of beer, explore craft beer production, and discover the fascinating world of small-scale craft brewing. Cheers to your brewing adventures!

Exploring Unique Flavors and Ingredients

One of the most exciting aspects of beer production is the opportunity to experiment with unique flavors and ingredients. In this subchapter, we will dive into the world of brewing and explore how you can create beers that stand out from the crowd.

Craft beer production techniques have opened up a whole new world of possibilities for brewers. With an emphasis on creativity and quality, craft brewers have pushed the boundaries of what beer can be. They have introduced a wide range of unique flavors and ingredients, from exotic fruits and spices to unconventional grains and herbs. We will explore these techniques and show you how to incorporate them into your own brewing process.

For home brewing beginners, exploring unique flavors and ingredients can be a fun and rewarding experience. It allows you to unleash your creativity and develop your own signature brews. We will provide you with a step-by-step guide on how to get started, including tips on ingredient selection, recipe formulation, and brewing techniques.

Sour beers have gained popularity in recent years, with their tangy and acidic flavors. We will delve into the fascinating world of sour beer production and guide you through the process of creating your own mouth-puckering brews.

Traditional brewing methods from around the world offer a rich tapestry of flavors and ingredients. We will take you on a journey across continents, exploring the unique brewing techniques and ingredients used in different cultures. From Belgian Trappist ales to German lagers, you will discover the secrets behind these time-honored traditions.

For those with dietary restrictions, gluten-free beer production has become a game-changer. We will explore the various grains and techniques that can be used to produce delicious gluten-free beers, allowing you to enjoy the flavors of beer without compromising your health.

Barrel-aged beer production offers a depth of flavor that is unparalleled. We will guide you through the process of aging beer in barrels, providing tips on selecting the right barrels and managing the aging process to achieve the desired flavor profile.

Fruit-infused beer brewing is another way to introduce unique flavors to your brews. We will share techniques for incorporating fruits into your beer, from fresh fruits to juices and purees, allowing you to create refreshing and aromatic brews.

Low-alcohol or non-alcoholic beer production has witnessed a surge in popularity as more people seek healthier alternatives. We will explore the techniques and ingredients used in brewing low-alcohol or non-alcoholic beers, providing you with a range of options to choose from.

Brewing seasonal or holiday beers is a tradition that many beer drinkers look forward to. We will provide you with recipes and ideas for brewing beers that capture the essence of each season or holiday, from spiced winter ales to refreshing summer lagers.

Finally, we will delve into the art of beer pairing and provide you with food recipes that complement different beer styles. Whether you enjoy a hearty stout with a rich chocolate dessert or a crisp IPA with spicy Mexican cuisine, we will help you discover the perfect beer and food combinations.

In this subchapter, we invite you to embark on a journey of exploration and experimentation. With a wide range of flavors and ingredients to choose from, you have the power to create unique and unforgettable beers that will delight your taste buds and impress your friends. So, let's raise a glass to the endless possibilities of brewing!

Experimenting with Hop Varieties

Hops play a crucial role in the flavor, aroma, and bitterness of beer. They are responsible for adding that distinctive hoppy character that beer drinkers love. However, with so many hop varieties available, it can be overwhelming to choose the right one for your brew. That's where experimenting with hop varieties comes in.

In this subchapter, we will explore the exciting world of hop varieties and how you can use them to create different kinds of beer. Whether you are a beginner or an experienced homebrewer, understanding hop varieties will take your beer production to the next level.

First, we will delve into the characteristics of different hop varieties. From the citrusy and floral notes of Cascade hops to the piney and resinous flavors of Simcoe hops, each variety has its unique profile. We will provide a comprehensive guide to the most popular hop varieties and explain their flavor and aroma profiles. This information will help you make informed decisions when selecting hops for your brew.

Next, we will discuss the importance of hop utilization and timing. Hops can be added at different stages of the brewing process, such as during the boil, whirlpool, or dry hopping. We will explain how each method affects the final flavor and aroma of the beer. Additionally, we will provide tips on hop storage and handling to ensure freshness and maximum flavor extraction.

Furthermore, we will explore the art of hop blending. By combining different hop varieties, you can create unique flavor profiles that suit your taste preferences. We will share recipes and techniques for hop blending, allowing you to experiment with different combinations and create your signature brew.

Finally, we will discuss the emerging trends in hop varieties, such as experimental hops and hop breeding programs. These new varieties offer exciting and unexpected flavors that push the boundaries of traditional brewing. We will provide insights into these innovative hops and how you can incorporate them into your beer production.

Whether you are interested in brewing hop-forward IPAs, floral pale ales, or balanced lagers, experimenting with hop varieties is essential. This subchapter will equip you with the knowledge and techniques to confidently select, use, and blend hops to create a wide range of beer styles. So grab a pint, and let's dive into the world of hop experimentation!

Barrel-Aging Techniques

Barrel-aging is a time-honored tradition in the beer world that adds depth, complexity, and unique flavors to your brew. Whether you are a homebrewer looking to experiment or a craft beer enthusiast eager to learn more, understanding barrel-aging techniques is essential. In this subchapter, we will delve into the art of barrel-aging and explore the various methods involved.

Firstly, it's important to choose the right type of barrel for your beer. Traditionally, oak barrels have been the go-to choice due to their porous nature, allowing for oxygen exchange and the extraction of flavors from the wood. However, brewers have also been experimenting with other types of barrels, such as bourbon, whiskey, or wine barrels, to lend distinct flavors to their brews.

Once you have selected your barrel, the next step is to properly prepare it. This involves cleaning and sanitizing the barrel to prevent any unwanted bacteria or off-flavors from contaminating your beer. Additionally, you may want to consider "seasoning" the barrel by filling it with water or a low-alcohol beer to expand the wood's fibers and remove any harsh flavors.

When it comes to aging your beer in the barrel, there are two primary methods: direct aging and blending. Direct aging involves transferring your beer directly into the barrel, allowing it to interact with the wood and absorb its unique characteristics. This method is ideal for bold, robust beers like stouts or barleywines.

On the other hand, blending involves mixing barrel-aged beer with fresh beer to achieve a desired flavor profile. This technique allows for more control over the final product and is often used in sour beer production. Blending can create a harmonious balance between the acidity and sweetness of the beer, resulting in a complex and refreshing brew.

During the aging process, it's important to monitor the beer regularly. Sampling the beer at different stages will help you determine when it has reached its optimal flavor. Factors such as temperature, humidity, and time will all influence the final outcome, so patience and attention to detail are key.

Once your beer has reached its desired level of barrel-aging, it's time to package and enjoy your creation. Whether you choose to bottle or keg your beer, be sure to store it properly to maintain its unique flavors and aromas.

In conclusion, barrel-aging techniques offer beer drinkers a world of possibilities. From the rich, velvety notes imparted by oak barrels to the subtle nuances of whiskey or wine casks, barrel-aging can elevate your beer to new heights. So, grab a barrel, experiment, and let your creativity flow as you uncover the art of barrel-aging in your brewing journey. Cheers!

Souring Methods and Wild Fermentation

In the world of beer production, there are countless techniques and methods that brewers can utilize to create unique and flavorful brews. One such technique that has gained popularity in recent years is souring methods and wild fermentation. This subchapter will delve into the fascinating world of sour beer production and the art of wild fermentation.

Sour beers, known for their tart and acidic flavors, are a favorite among beer enthusiasts looking for something a little different. These beers are typically brewed using a combination of traditional brewing methods and a process called souring. Souring involves intentionally introducing certain bacteria and wild yeasts into the beer during fermentation, resulting in the distinct sour taste.

There are several methods that brewers can employ to achieve sourness in their beers. One popular method is known as kettle souring. In this process, the wort is boiled and then cooled before being inoculated with lactobacillus bacteria. The bacteria feast on the sugars in the wort, producing lactic acid and giving the beer its sour character. The soured wort is then boiled again to kill off any remaining bacteria before yeast is added for fermentation.

Another method, known as barrel aging, involves aging the beer in wooden barrels that have been previously inoculated with wild yeasts and bacteria. Over time, the beer picks up the unique flavors and characteristics of the microorganisms present in the barrel, resulting in a complex and sour beer.

Wild fermentation is another technique that can be used to create sour beers. In this method, brewers rely on the natural yeasts and bacteria present in the environment to ferment the beer. This can lead to unpredictable and ever-changing flavors, making each batch of beer truly unique.

While sour beers may not be for everyone, they offer a wide range of flavor profiles and can be a delightful departure from the more traditional styles. Whether you're a seasoned beer drinker or just starting out on your brewing journey, experimenting with souring methods and wild fermentation can open up a whole new world of possibilities.

In the next chapter, we will explore traditional brewing methods from around the world, giving you a glimpse into the rich history and cultural significance of beer production. So grab a pint, sit back, and get ready to embark on a flavorful journey through the world of beer!

Fruit and Spice Infusions

One of the most exciting aspects of beer production is the opportunity to experiment with different flavors and ingredients. Fruit and spice infusions offer a fantastic way to add a unique twist to your brews and tantalize your taste buds. In this subchapter, we will explore the art of infusing beer with various fruits and spices, allowing you to create a truly exceptional drinking experience.

When it comes to fruit-infused beers, the possibilities are endless. From citrusy oranges and zesty lemons to sweet berries and tropical pineapples, the fruit infusion can elevate your beer to a whole new level. Not only do these fruits add a burst of flavor, but they also contribute natural sugars that can ferment, resulting in a higher alcohol content.

But it's not just about the fruits; spices can also play a significant role in beer production. Spices like cinnamon, nutmeg, cloves, and ginger can bring warmth and complexity to your brews, making them perfect for holiday or seasonal beers. You can even experiment with more unconventional spices such as cardamom, coriander, or even chili peppers to add an unexpected twist to your creations.

When it comes to infusing beer with fruits and spices, timing is crucial. You can add the ingredients during different stages of the brewing process, such as during the boil, fermentation, or aging. Each method will yield a different flavor profile, so it's essential to experiment and find what works best for your desired outcome.

Additionally, it's important to consider the beer style when deciding which fruits and spices to use. Some styles, like wheat beers or pale ales, pair exceptionally well with citrusy fruits, while darker beers like stouts or porters can be complemented by rich, dark fruits like cherries or plums. The key is to find a balance that enhances the beer's natural flavors without overpowering them.

In this subchapter, we will delve into the different techniques and considerations for fruit and spice infusions. We will guide you through the process of selecting the right ingredients, preparing them for infusion, and incorporating them into your brews. Furthermore, we will provide you with tried-and-true recipes and tips for achieving the perfect balance of flavors.

Whether you're a homebrewer looking to experiment with new flavors or a craft beer enthusiast seeking to expand your knowledge, fruit and spice infusions offer an exciting avenue to explore. Get ready to embark on a flavor-filled journey and unlock a whole new world of brewing possibilities. Cheers to creating truly unique and delicious beers!

Chapter 4: Home Brewing for Beginners

Getting Started with Home Brewing

If you are a beer drinker who has always been fascinated by the art of producing different kinds of beer, then home brewing might be the perfect hobby for you. Not only does it give you the opportunity to create your own unique flavors and experiment with various ingredients, but it also allows you to gain a deeper appreciation for the craft beer industry. In this subchapter, we will guide you through the process of getting started with home brewing.

Before diving into the world of home brewing, it is important to understand the basics. Craft beer production techniques are the foundation of any successful home brewing endeavor. Familiarize yourself with the ingredients used in brewing, such as malt, hops, yeast, and water. Learn about the different types of grains and hops available and how they contribute to the overall flavor profile.

For beginners, it is recommended to start with a simple beer recipe. Brewing sour beers or using traditional brewing methods from around the world can be complex and require advanced skills. Instead, opt for a basic recipe that will allow you to get a grasp of the brewing process without overwhelming you with complicated steps.

Gluten-free beer production has gained popularity in recent years, catering to those with gluten sensitivities. If you or someone you know falls into this category, explore the techniques and ingredients used in gluten-free brewing.

Barrel-aged beer production and fruit-infused beer brewing are techniques that can add depth and complexity to your brews. Experiment with different types of barrels, such as oak or whiskey barrels, to impart unique flavors. Likewise, try adding fruits like berries, citrus, or even tropical fruits to infuse your beer with a burst of flavor.

For those looking for healthier options or seeking to reduce alcohol consumption, low-alcohol or non-alcoholic beer production is a great alternative. Discover techniques that allow you to create flavorful, yet low-alcohol or alcohol-free beers.

Brewing seasonal or holiday beers can be a fun and festive way to celebrate special occasions. Experiment with spices, fruits, and other seasonal ingredients to create beers that capture the essence of the season.

Finally, beer pairing and food recipes are essential to enhance your overall beer-drinking experience. Learn about the art of pairing different beer styles with various foods to create harmonious flavor combinations.

Home brewing is a journey that allows you to unleash your creativity and explore the vast world of beer production. With the right knowledge and techniques, you can take your love for beer to the next level and produce your very own unique brews. So, grab your brewing equipment and get ready to embark on an exciting brewing adventure!

Essential Equipment for Home Brewers

Home brewing has become a popular hobby for beer enthusiasts all over the world. With the right equipment, anyone can produce their own delicious beer right in the comfort of their own home. Whether you're a beginner or an experienced brewer, having the essential equipment is crucial to ensure the quality and success of your brews. In this subchapter, we will explore the must-have equipment for home brewers.

1. Brew kettle: A large stainless steel pot is essential for boiling your ingredients and creating the wort. Look for a kettle with a capacity of at least 5 gallons to accommodate different batch sizes.

2. Fermenter: A primary fermenter is where the magic happens. Choose between a plastic bucket or a glass carboy, both of which have their advantages. Make sure it has an airtight lid and an airlock to allow the release of carbon dioxide during fermentation.

3. Airlock and stopper: These small but crucial tools prevent any unwanted contaminants from entering the fermenter while still allowing carbon dioxide to escape.

4. Hydrometer: This device measures the specific gravity of your beer, helping you determine its alcohol content and fermentation progress. It is an essential tool for any brewer looking to fine-tune their recipes.

5. Auto-siphon: Transferring your beer from one vessel to another can be a messy process without an auto-siphon. This tool makes it easy to move your beer without introducing any air or contaminants.

6. Bottles and capper: Once your beer has finished fermenting, it's time to bottle it. Choose between glass or plastic bottles and invest in a quality capper to seal them properly.

7. Thermometer: Monitoring the temperature during the brewing process is crucial for achieving the desired flavors and avoiding any off-flavors. A digital thermometer will provide accurate readings.

8. Brewing spoon: A long-handled spoon is necessary for stirring your ingredients during the brewing process. Look for a stainless steel or heat-resistant plastic spoon.

9. Cleaning and sanitizing supplies: Keeping your equipment clean and sanitized is essential to prevent any contamination. Invest in a quality cleaning solution and sanitizer to maintain a safe brewing environment.

10. Recipe book or brewing software: While not a physical tool, having access to recipes and brewing software will help you create different kinds of beer and experiment with new flavors.

By equipping yourself with these essential tools, you'll be well on your way to becoming a successful home brewer. Remember, brewing beer is a process that requires patience and attention to detail, but with the right equipment and a passion for brewing, you'll be producing your own delicious beers in no time. Cheers!

Choosing the Right Ingredients

When it comes to producing different kinds of beer, the ingredients you use play a crucial role in determining the flavor, aroma, and overall quality of your brew. Whether you are a craft beer enthusiast, a homebrewing beginner, or just someone looking to experiment with different beer styles, understanding how to choose the right ingredients is essential.

One of the first things to consider is the type of malt you want to use. Malt is the backbone of beer and provides the necessary sugars for fermentation. Depending on the desired flavor profile, you can choose from a variety of malts, including pale malt for a light and crisp beer, roasted malt for a rich and dark brew, or specialty malts for unique flavors and aromas.

Next, you should select the hops. Hops not only add bitterness to balance the sweetness of the malt but also contribute to the aroma and flavor of the beer. Different hop varieties can bring citrusy, floral, piney, or earthy notes to your brew. Experimenting with different combinations of hops can help you create a beer that is truly unique and tailored to your taste.

Yeast is another crucial ingredient in beer production. It is responsible for fermentation, converting the sugars in the malt into alcohol and carbon dioxide. There are various strains of yeast available, each offering different flavors and characteristics. Ale yeast, for example, ferments at warmer temperatures and produces fruity and estery flavors, while lager yeast ferments at colder temperatures and creates a clean and crisp taste.

Additionally, water quality should not be overlooked. Water makes up the majority of beer, and its mineral content can affect the final product. Depending on the beer style, you may need to adjust the water chemistry to match the desired flavor profile. Some breweries even replicate the water composition of specific regions known for their beer styles, such as the soft water of Pilsen for brewing Czech Pilsners.

Lastly, adjuncts and flavorings can be added to enhance the beer's character. This includes fruits, spices, herbs, and even barrel aging. These ingredients can add complexity and depth to your brew, allowing you to experiment with different flavors and create unique beer experiences.

Choosing the right ingredients is a fundamental step in producing different kinds of beer. By understanding the characteristics of each ingredient and experimenting with different combinations, you can craft beers that satisfy your taste preferences and impress your friends. So, go ahead, let your creativity flow, and enjoy the journey of brewing your very own masterpiece. Cheers!

Step-by-Step Home Brewing Process

For beer enthusiasts who are eager to explore the world of craft beer production, home brewing is the perfect way to unleash your creativity and customize your brews to suit your taste preferences. In this subchapter, we will guide you through the step-by-step process of home brewing, helping you produce your very own high-quality beer right in the comfort of your own home.

1. Gathering Equipment: Before you start the brewing process, it is essential to gather all the necessary equipment. This includes a fermenting vessel, airlock, thermometer, hydrometer, brewing kettle, and sanitizing solution. Ensuring that your equipment is properly cleaned and sanitized is crucial to avoid any contamination.

2. Selecting Your Ingredients: The heart of any beer is the ingredients. You have the freedom to experiment with various malt, hops, yeast, and water profiles to create unique flavors. Research different recipes and select the ingredients that align with the style of beer you wish to produce.

3. Mashing: This is the process where the enzymes in the malt convert starches into sugars. Heat water to a specific temperature and add crushed malt to create a mash. Allow it to rest for a specific duration to extract the desired sugars and flavors.

4. Boiling and Hopping: After mashing, transfer the liquid (wort) to a brewing kettle and bring it to a boil. Add hops at different intervals to achieve the desired bitterness, flavor, and aroma. The boiling process also sterilizes the wort.

5. Fermentation: Once the boiling is complete, cool the wort to the appropriate temperature and transfer it to a sanitized fermenting vessel. Add yeast and seal the vessel with an airlock. The yeast will consume the sugars, converting them into alcohol and carbon dioxide, resulting in the formation of beer.

6. Conditioning and Carbonation: After fermentation, the beer needs to condition to develop its flavors and clarify. Transfer the beer to a secondary vessel, known as a carboy, and allow it to age for a specific

period. Carbonation can be achieved naturally through the addition of priming sugar or by force carbonation methods.

7. Bottling and Enjoyment: Finally, it's time to bottle your beer. Clean and sanitize your bottles and carefully transfer the beer, being cautious not to introduce any oxygen. Seal the bottles and store them in a cool, dark place for proper carbonation. After a few weeks, your beer will be ready to be enjoyed!

Home brewing is an art that can be mastered with practice and experimentation. By following this step-by-step process, you will be well on your way to producing your own delicious, handcrafted beer. So, gather your ingredients, fire up your kettle, and embark on this exciting journey of home brewing! Cheers to your brewing success!

Troubleshooting Tips for Home Brewers

Home brewing is an exciting and rewarding hobby that allows beer enthusiasts to create their own unique brews. However, like any craft, it can come with its fair share of challenges. In this subchapter, we will cover some troubleshooting tips to help home brewers overcome common issues and achieve the best possible results in their beer production.

1. Off-flavors and Aromas: One of the most common problems faced by home brewers is the presence of off-flavors or undesirable aromas in their beer. This can be caused by various factors such as improper sanitization, fermentation temperature, or aging process. To troubleshoot this issue, it is crucial to maintain proper sanitation throughout the brewing process, control fermentation temperatures within the recommended range, and allow enough time for the beer to age and mature.

2. Cloudy Beer: If your beer turns out cloudy instead of clear, it may be due to several reasons. Poorly crushed grains, incomplete or improper

filtration, or excessive sediment can all contribute to this issue. To resolve it, ensure that your grains are properly crushed, improve your filtration system, and consider using fining agents or cold crashing techniques to clarify the beer.

3. Low Carbonation: If your beer lacks carbonation or has a flat taste, the problem could lie in the priming process or the fermentation itself. Make sure to calculate the correct amount of priming sugar and mix it thoroughly into the beer before bottling. Additionally, ensure that the fermentation process is complete before bottling, as incomplete fermentation can result in undercarbonated beer.

4. High Alcohol Content: If your beer turns out to be higher in alcohol than intended, it could be due to a few factors such as incorrect measurements or miscalculations in the brewing process. Double-check your recipe and measurements to ensure accuracy, and consider adjusting the amounts of fermentables used in subsequent batches.

5. Infection: Infection is a common concern in home brewing and can lead to off-flavors and other issues. Proper sanitation and cleanliness throughout the brewing process are essential to avoid contamination. Thoroughly clean and sanitize all equipment, including fermenters, airlocks, and tubing, and consider using a sanitizer specifically designed for brewing purposes.

By following these troubleshooting tips, home brewers can overcome common challenges and produce high-quality, delicious beers. Remember, brewing is a learning process, and even experienced brewers face setbacks from time to time. With practice and perseverance, you can refine your skills and create exceptional brews that will impress both yourself and your fellow beer enthusiasts. Cheers to your brewing journey!

Scaling Up Your Homebrew

For the passionate beer drinker who has mastered the art of homebrewing, it's only natural to want to take your craft to the next level. Scaling up your homebrew allows you to produce larger quantities of beer, experiment with new ingredients and techniques, and share your creations with a wider audience. In this subchapter, we will explore the various aspects of scaling up your homebrew and provide you with practical tips and advice to ensure your success.

One of the first considerations when scaling up your homebrew is equipment. As you increase your production volume, you'll need larger fermenters, brew kettles, and storage vessels. Investing in quality equipment that can handle larger batches is essential to maintaining the integrity and consistency of your beer.

Next, you'll need to adjust your recipe to accommodate the larger batch size. Scaling up a recipe involves calculating the new quantities of ingredients, such as malt, hops, yeast, and water. It's important to maintain the correct ratios and proportions to achieve the desired flavor profile. We will walk you through the process of scaling up your recipes and provide you with helpful tools and formulas to simplify the calculations.

Scaling up your homebrew also requires careful consideration of the fermentation process. Larger batches may require more precise temperature control and monitoring to ensure optimal fermentation conditions. We will discuss different fermentation techniques and equipment options to help you maintain the quality and consistency of your beer.

Furthermore, we will delve into the logistics of scaling up your homebrew operation. From sourcing ingredients in larger quantities to managing inventory and storage, we will guide you through the practical aspects of producing larger batches of beer.

Finally, we will touch on the topic of scaling up your homebrew business. If your passion for brewing extends beyond your personal enjoyment, we will provide insights into the steps to take when transitioning from a hobbyist to a professional brewer. This includes licensing requirements, marketing strategies, and considerations for distribution and sales.

Whether you're a beer enthusiast looking to produce larger quantities of your favorite brew or an aspiring professional brewer, scaling up your homebrew is an exciting and challenging endeavor. With our comprehensive guide, you'll have the knowledge and confidence to take your homebrewing to new heights and share your creations with the world. Cheers to scaling up and enjoying the fruits of your labor!

Chapter 5: Brewing Sour Beers

Introduction to Sour Beers

Sour beers, with their tangy and acidic flavors, have gained immense popularity in recent years among beer enthusiasts. While traditional beer styles are known for their balanced and hoppy or malty profiles, sour beers offer a unique and refreshing experience that appeals to a wide range of palates. In this subchapter, we will delve into the fascinating world of sour beers, exploring their history, production techniques, and the various styles that exist.

Sour beers have a long and storied history, dating back centuries. Originating in Belgium, where they are still highly revered, these beers were initially created by accident when wild yeast and bacteria contaminated the brewing process. Over time, brewers learned to harness these microorganisms to intentionally create sour beers, thus giving rise to a distinct beer style.

One of the key characteristics of sour beers is their tartness, which is achieved through a process called souring. This process involves the introduction of specific strains of bacteria, such as Lactobacillus or Pediococcus, during fermentation. These bacteria produce lactic acid, resulting in the characteristic sour taste. Some sour beers also undergo a secondary fermentation with Brettanomyces yeast, adding complexity and unique flavors.

There are several styles of sour beers, each with its own distinct flavor profile. Lambic, Gueuze, Berliner Weisse, and Flanders Red Ale are just a few examples. Lambic beers are spontaneously fermented using wild yeast and bacteria, while Gueuze is a blend of young and aged Lambics. Berliner Weisse is a light and refreshing sour beer, often enjoyed with fruit syrups, while Flanders Red Ale exhibits complex flavors of fruit, oak, and acidity.

Producing sour beers requires careful attention to brewing techniques, as well as the selection of specific yeast and bacteria strains. While traditional brewing methods can be utilized, some brewers opt for barrel aging or blending techniques to enhance the sourness and complexity of the beer. The use of fruits, such as cherries or raspberries, is also common in sour beer production, adding a delightful fruity twist to the tart base.

For those interested in brewing their own sour beers, it is essential to understand the importance of sanitation and the potential risks associated with introducing wild yeast and bacteria into the brewing process. However, with proper knowledge and techniques, home brewers can create their own unique and flavorful sour beers, tailored to their preferences.

Whether you are a seasoned beer enthusiast or new to the world of craft brewing, sour beers offer a delightful departure from traditional beer styles. Their complex and tangy flavors, coupled with the variety of styles and brewing techniques, make sour beers an exciting and ever-evolving category in the world of craft beer. So, grab a glass and prepare to embark on a sour beer adventure that will tantalize your taste buds and expand your appreciation for the rich diversity of beer. Cheers!

Souring Techniques and Microorganisms

One of the most fascinating aspects of beer production is the use of souring techniques and microorganisms to create unique and complex flavors. These techniques have been employed by brewers around the world for centuries, and they continue to be a popular choice among craft beer enthusiasts. In this subchapter, we will explore the different souring techniques and the microorganisms responsible for creating these delightful sour beers.

Sour beers are known for their tart and acidic taste, which is achieved through a process called souring. There are several different methods to achieve this sourness, including the use of specific microorganisms or the addition of souring agents. One of the most common techniques is spontaneous fermentation, where wild yeast and bacteria present in the environment are allowed to ferment the beer. This method is commonly used in traditional brewing methods from around the world, such as Belgian lambics and gueuze.

Another popular method is the addition of specific microorganisms, such as lactobacillus or pediococcus, which are known for their ability to produce lactic acid. These bacteria thrive in an anaerobic environment and can be added during the brewing process to achieve the desired sourness. This technique is often used in American sour ales and Berliner Weissbiers.

Different strains of yeast and bacteria can also be used in combination to create complex flavors and aromas. For example, the addition of Brettanomyces yeast can add funky and fruity notes to the beer, while lactobacillus can contribute a refreshing tartness. These combinations allow brewers to experiment with different flavor profiles and create truly unique and innovative sour beers.

It is important to note that souring techniques require careful monitoring and control to prevent off-flavors or excessive acidity. Brewers must have a thorough understanding of the microorganisms involved and the optimal conditions for their growth. This includes controlling the temperature, pH levels, and oxygen exposure during the fermentation process.

In recent years, the popularity of sour beers has skyrocketed, with craft breweries around the world embracing these funky and refreshing styles. Home brewers are also getting in on the action, experimenting with different souring techniques and microorganisms in their own brewing setups. The possibilities are endless, and the only limit is your imagination.

So, if you're a beer drinker interested in expanding your palate and exploring new flavors, sour beers are definitely worth a try. Whether you prefer the traditional lambics of Belgium or the bold American sour ales, there is a sour beer out there for everyone. Cheers to the wonderful world of souring techniques and the microorganisms that make it all possible!

Traditional Sour Beer Styles

Sour beers have gained significant popularity in recent years, appealing to beer enthusiasts seeking unique and complex flavors. These beers have a long history, with traditional brewing methods from around the world contributing to their distinct taste profiles. In this subchapter, we will explore the diverse range of traditional sour beer styles and the techniques used to produce them.

One of the most well-known traditional sour beer styles is Lambic. Originating from the Pajottenland region of Belgium, Lambic is the result of spontaneous fermentation using wild yeasts and bacteria present in the air. This ancient brewing method gives Lambic its characteristic tart, funky, and often fruity flavors. Gueuze, a blend of young and aged Lambic, further enhances the complexity and effervescence of this style.

Another traditional sour beer style is Berliner Weisse, hailing from Germany. This wheat-based beer is typically low in alcohol and known for its refreshing, sour, and slightly acidic taste. Traditionally, Berliner

Weisse is often served with flavored syrup, such as raspberry or woodruff, allowing drinkers to adjust the sweetness to their liking.

Flamish Red Ale, originating from Flanders, Belgium, is another traditional sour beer style worth mentioning. This style is aged in oak barrels, contributing to its unique flavors of tart cherries, red wine, and oak. The use of mixed fermentation involving both traditional brewer's yeast and wild yeasts adds depth and complexity to this beer.

In addition to these traditional sour beer styles, there are many other regional variations worth exploring. The American wild ale, for example, draws inspiration from traditional sour beers but incorporates local ingredients and innovative brewing techniques. The result is a wide range of flavors, from fruity and tart to funky and earthy.

Whether you are an experienced beer drinker or a homebrewing enthusiast, experimenting with traditional sour beer styles can offer a delightful journey into the world of complex flavors. By understanding the traditional brewing methods and techniques behind these styles, you can create your own unique sour beers that will impress both yourself and your friends.

In the following chapters of this book, we will delve further into the craft beer production techniques, home brewing for beginners, and brewing sour beers. Stay tuned to discover the secrets behind producing different kinds of beer, including traditional sour beer styles, and elevate your brewing skills to new heights. Cheers!

Sour Beer Recipes and Variations

If you're a beer lover who enjoys exploring unique flavors and styles, then sour beers are an absolute must-try. These beers have gained popularity in recent years for their distinct tartness and complex flavors. In this subchapter, we will delve into the world of sour beer production, providing you with recipes and variations that will tantalize your taste buds.

1. Traditional Sour Beer Recipes:

- Belgian Lambic: This traditional Belgian beer is spontaneously fermented using wild yeast and bacteria, resulting in a complex, sour flavor profile. It can be aged for several years, developing deeper flavors over time.

- Berliner Weisse: Originating from Germany, this light and refreshing beer is brewed with a blend of yeast and lactic acid bacteria. It is often served with a flavored syrup, such as raspberry or woodruff, to balance the tartness.

2. Fruit-Infused Sour Beers:

- Raspberry Sour: Add fresh or frozen raspberries to a basic sour beer recipe during fermentation for a burst of fruity goodness. The natural sweetness of the berries complements the sourness, creating a delightful balance.

- Cherry Lambic: Ferment your lambic with cherries to create a vibrant red beer with a tart and sweet flavor profile. This beer is a popular choice for special occasions and pairs well with rich desserts.

3. Barrel-Aged Sour Beers:

- Flanders Red Ale: This beer style is aged in oak barrels, allowing it to develop a deep, rich flavor profile with notes of caramel, oak, and sourness. It is typically a blend of young and aged beers, creating a complex and balanced final product.

- Bourbon Barrel-Aged Sour: Take your favorite sour beer recipe and age it in bourbon barrels for several months. The result is a tantalizing combination of sourness, oak, and subtle bourbon flavors.

4. Low-Alcohol or Non-Alcoholic Sour Beers:

- Kombucha Beer: Brew a kombucha base and then ferment it with a sour beer yeast strain to create a low-alcohol or non-alcoholic sour beer. This refreshing option is perfect for those looking for a lighter alternative.

These are just a few examples of the endless possibilities when it comes to brewing sour beers. Whether you prefer traditional recipes, fruit-infused variations, barrel-aged complexities, or low-alcohol options, there is a sour beer recipe out there to suit your taste. So grab your brewing equipment, experiment with different ingredients, and embark on a sour beer brewing adventure that will leave you craving more. Cheers to the wonderful world of sour beers!

Aging and Blending Sour Beers

Sour beers have gained immense popularity among beer enthusiasts in recent years. Their unique and complex flavors, often characterized by tartness and acidity, offer a refreshing departure from the more traditional beer styles. But what sets sour beers apart from their counterparts? The answer lies in the aging and blending process.

Aging sour beers is a labor of love that requires patience and a keen understanding of the brewing process. Unlike other beer styles, which are typically consumed fresh, sour beers undergo a secondary fermentation process that can take months or even years. During this time, a microbial cocktail of bacteria and wild yeast transforms the beer, imparting those signature sour flavors.

The aging process begins with the primary fermentation, where the brewer introduces a select strain of bacteria or wild yeast into the wort. These microorganisms, such as lactobacillus or Brettanomyces, consume the sugars and produce lactic acid or acetic acid, giving the beer its sour taste. After primary fermentation, the beer is transferred to barrels or other aging vessels, where it continues to develop and mature.

Blending is another crucial step in the production of sour beers. Brewers often create a blend of different aged beers to achieve the desired flavor profile. This artful process allows them to balance acidity, funkiness, and other complex flavors. By combining beers aged for varying lengths of time, brewers can create a harmonious blend that showcases the best qualities of each component.

The practice of aging and blending sour beers is not limited to commercial breweries. Homebrewers can also experiment with these techniques to create their own unique sour brews. While the process may require some additional equipment and a longer timeframe, the end result can be truly rewarding.

Whether you're a seasoned beer drinker or just starting to explore the world of craft brewing, aging and blending sour beers offers a fascinating journey into the realm of flavor experimentation. So, next time you come across a sour beer, take a moment to appreciate the craftsmanship and artistry that goes into producing these complex and delicious brews. And who knows, you might even be inspired to try your hand at brewing your own sour masterpiece. Cheers!

Tips for Achieving Balance in Sour Beers

Sour beers have gained significant popularity among beer enthusiasts in recent years, thanks to their unique and complex flavor profiles. However, achieving the perfect balance in sour beers can be a challenging task for brewers. In this subchapter, we will explore some tips that will help you produce well-balanced and delicious sour beers that will leave your taste buds craving for more.

1. Start with a Solid Base Beer: The foundation of any great sour beer is a well-brewed base beer. Choose a beer style that complements the

souring process and has a solid malt and hop profile. This will provide a sturdy backbone for the souring agents to work their magic.

2. Choose the Right Souring Agent: There are various ways to sour a beer, including spontaneous fermentation, adding wild yeasts, or using specific bacteria strains like lactobacillus or pediococcus. Experiment with different souring agents to find the one that suits your taste preferences and desired flavor profile.

3. Control the Souring Process: Souring can take anywhere from a few days to several months, depending on the desired level of acidity. It's crucial to monitor the pH levels throughout the process to ensure you don't end up with an overly tart or undrinkable beer. Consider investing in a pH meter to accurately measure the acidity.

4. Blend for Balance: If your sour beer turns out too tart or acidic, don't despair. Blending can be a great tool for achieving balance. Mix different batches of sour beer with varying levels of acidity to create a final product that hits the perfect sweet spot.

5. Experiment with Fruit Additions: Fruit-infused sour beers can add a delightful complexity and balance to the tartness. Experiment with different fruits, such as cherries, raspberries, or peaches, to find the perfect combination that complements the sourness.

6. Consider Aging in Oak Barrels: Barrel aging can add depth and complexity to sour beers. Oak barrels impart unique flavors and can help mellow out the acidity over time. Experiment with different types of barrels, such as wine or whiskey barrels, to create new flavor profiles.

7. Seek Inspiration from Traditional Brewing Methods: Look to traditional brewing methods from around the world to gain insight into achieving balance in sour beers. Learn from the brewing techniques of Belgian Lambics or German Berliner Weisse, which have a long-standing history of producing exceptional sour beers.

Remember, achieving balance in sour beers requires patience, experimentation, and a keen understanding of the brewing process. By following these tips, you'll be well on your way to producing sour beers that will impress even the most discerning beer drinkers. Cheers to your brewing adventures!

Chapter 6: Traditional Brewing Methods from Around the World

Traditional Brewing Techniques in Europe

Europe has a rich history when it comes to brewing beer, with each country having its own unique brewing techniques and styles. In this subchapter, we will explore the traditional brewing techniques that have been passed down through generations in Europe.

One of the most well-known brewing techniques in Europe is the Reinheitsgebot, also known as the German Beer Purity Law. This law, dating back to 1516, states that beer can only be brewed using water, barley, and hops. This technique ensures that the beer produced is of high quality and free from any additives or preservatives.

Belgium is famous for its Trappist beers, which are brewed by monks in monasteries. These beers are typically made using traditional methods, with the fermentation process taking place in oak barrels. The monks have perfected their brewing techniques over centuries, resulting in unique and flavorful beers.

In England, the traditional brewing technique of cask conditioning is still widely practiced. This involves the fermentation and conditioning of beer in casks, allowing the flavors to develop naturally. The beer is then served directly from the cask, providing a distinct taste and texture.

In Ireland, the traditional brewing technique of dry stout production is prevalent. This involves the use of roasted barley, which gives the beer its distinctive dark color and rich flavor. The beer is brewed using a combination of malted barley, hops, water, and yeast, resulting in a smooth and creamy stout.

Another traditional brewing technique found in Europe is the use of wild yeasts in the production of sour beers. This technique is commonly used in Belgium, where beers such as Lambic and Gueuze are brewed. The wild yeasts present in the air and the barrels contribute to the unique flavors and tartness of these beers.

These traditional brewing techniques have stood the test of time and continue to be practiced by breweries across Europe. Whether you're a beer connoisseur or a home brewer, exploring these techniques will provide you with a deeper understanding and appreciation for the art of brewing. So, raise your glass and savor the flavors of Europe's traditional brews!

Exploring Asian Beer Styles

When it comes to beer, most people automatically think of classic European varieties like lagers and ales. However, there is a whole world of beer styles out there waiting to be discovered, and Asia has its own unique and exciting contributions to offer. In this subchapter, we will delve into the fascinating world of Asian beer styles and explore the flavors and techniques that make them so distinct.

Asia is a diverse continent with a rich cultural heritage, and this is reflected in its beer traditions. From the light and refreshing lagers of Japan to the complex and spicy brews of India, there is something to suit every palate. One of the standout styles is Japanese rice beer, which is brewed using a combination of malted barley and rice. This gives the beer a clean and crisp flavor, making it perfect for pairing with sushi or other Japanese cuisine.

Moving on to China, we find another unique beer style known as baijiu. This traditional Chinese beer is made using a fermentation process that involves both barley and sorghum, resulting in a slightly sweet and fruity flavor. Baijiu is often enjoyed on special occasions and is a staple at Chinese New Year celebrations.

Venturing further south, we come across the rich and aromatic beers of India. Known for their bold flavors and high alcohol content, Indian beers are a true sensory experience. The famous India Pale Ale (IPA) style originated during the British colonial era when hops were added to the beer to preserve it during long voyages from England to India. This led to the development of a unique hoppy and bitter flavor profile that is now synonymous with the IPA style.

In addition to these well-known styles, Asia is also home to a variety of lesser-known but equally intriguing beer traditions. From the tangy and tart Korean rice beer called makgeolli to the earthy and herbal Tibetan barley beer called chang, there is no shortage of exciting flavors to explore.

As a beer drinker, expanding your horizons and exploring Asian beer styles can be a rewarding and enjoyable experience. Whether you're a craft beer enthusiast, a homebrewing beginner, or simply someone looking to try something new, Asian beer styles offer a whole world of flavors waiting to be discovered. So why not embark on a beer-tasting journey through Asia and experience the diverse and vibrant beer cultures of this fascinating continent?

African and South American Brewing Traditions

In this subchapter, we delve into the rich brewing traditions of Africa and South America, where beer has been an integral part of their cultures for centuries. These regions have unique brewing techniques and ingredients that add a distinct flavor profile to their beers.

Starting with Africa, we find a wide range of traditional brewing methods passed down through generations. One such technique is the use of sorghum, millet, or maize as the base ingredient for brewing.

These grains, often malted and fermented, produce beers with a rich, earthy taste and a slightly sour note. The local communities in Africa have perfected these recipes over time, resulting in a diverse range of flavors and aromas.

Moving on to South America, we encounter the ancient Andean brewing tradition that dates back thousands of years. Chicha, a fermented corn-based beverage, is a prominent example of this tradition. This beer-like concoction is made by chewing corn kernels to activate enzymes that convert starches into sugars, which are then fermented using wild yeast. This labor-intensive process imparts a unique sweetness and fruity flavor to the final product.

In both Africa and South America, brewing is often a communal activity, with entire villages coming together to brew large batches of beer for celebrations and ceremonies. This sense of community and shared knowledge is an integral part of their brewing traditions.

As beer enthusiasts, it is fascinating to explore these brewing techniques and learn how to incorporate them into our own craft beer production. By experimenting with traditional African and South American ingredients like sorghum, millet, maize, and corn, we can add a new dimension to our beer recipes.

Furthermore, understanding these ancient brewing methods can inspire us to explore new flavors and techniques in our homebrewing endeavors. Whether you are a beginner or an experienced homebrewer, incorporating these traditional brewing methods can elevate your craft and create truly unique beers.

In conclusion, African and South American brewing traditions offer a treasure trove of knowledge and inspiration for beer drinkers and enthusiasts. By embracing these techniques and ingredients, we can expand our repertoire of beer styles and create memorable brews that pay homage to these rich cultural heritages. So, grab a pint, and let's embark on a journey of discovery into the flavors and aromas of Africa and South America!

Indigenous Ingredients and Brewing Practices

Beer brewing is an art that has been practiced across the globe for centuries, with various cultures incorporating their unique flavors and brewing techniques. From the ancient Egyptians to the monks of Europe, each region has its own indigenous ingredients and brewing practices that contribute to the diversity of beer styles we enjoy today.

Exploring indigenous ingredients can add a new dimension to your beer production, creating distinctive flavors and aromas that will excite your taste buds. In this subchapter, we will delve into some of the fascinating ingredients and brewing practices from around the world.

One example is the use of unique grains like quinoa and millet in traditional brewing methods. These grains, which are indigenous to South America and Africa respectively, offer a gluten-free alternative to barley, allowing beer enthusiasts with dietary restrictions to enjoy their favorite beverage.

In addition to grains, various fruits, herbs, and spices have also been incorporated into beer recipes throughout history. For instance, the use of juniper berries in Nordic brewing produces a distinct and refreshing flavor. Similarly, the addition of prickly pear in Mexican brewing creates a vibrant and fruity character.

Understanding these indigenous ingredients and brewing practices can inspire you to experiment with new flavors and techniques in your own craft beer production. By incorporating these elements, you can create unique beers that stand out from the crowd and satisfy the taste buds of even the most discerning beer drinkers.

Furthermore, learning about traditional brewing methods from different cultures can provide valuable insights into the art of brewing. For example, the Belgian brewing tradition of spontaneous fermentation using open-air fermentation vessels called "coolships" contributes to the complex flavors found in lambic and gueuze beers.

Whether you are a homebrewing beginner or an experienced craft beer enthusiast, exploring indigenous ingredients and brewing practices will expand your knowledge and repertoire. This subchapter will equip you with the tools and inspiration to create beers that celebrate the rich cultural heritage of brewing around the world.

So, grab a pint, open your mind, and let's embark on a journey through the fascinating world of indigenous ingredients and brewing practices. Cheers!

Reviving Forgotten Beer Styles

In the ever-evolving world of craft beer, it's easy to get caught up in the latest trends and forget about the rich history and diversity of beer styles. That's why in this subchapter, we will delve into the art of reviving forgotten beer styles. As beer drinkers, it is essential to appreciate and explore the vast range of flavors and aromas that have been enjoyed for centuries.

Throughout history, many unique beer styles have fallen out of favor and into obscurity. However, with the increasing interest in traditional brewing methods and the craft beer revolution, there has been a renewed interest in resurrecting these forgotten gems. From ancient recipes to regional specialties, the possibilities are endless.

One such example is the Gose, a sour and slightly salty beer style originating from Germany. This once-forgotten brew has made a comeback in recent years, captivating beer enthusiasts with its tangy and refreshing flavor profile. By understanding the traditional brewing techniques and experimenting with modern variations, you too can revive this forgotten style.

Another forgotten beer style worth exploring is the Grätzer, a smoked wheat beer from Poland. Once popular in the 18th century, this unique brew was nearly wiped out during World War II. However, with the help of passionate brewers and historical research, the Grätzer is making a comeback. Learn how to recreate this smoky and complex beer using traditional ingredients and techniques.

Reviving forgotten beer styles is not just about preserving history; it's about pushing the boundaries of flavor and creativity. By studying old recipes and experimenting with modern ingredients, you can create unique and exciting beers that pay homage to the past while embracing the present.

In this subchapter, we will guide you through the process of reviving forgotten beer styles step by step. From researching historical recipes to sourcing authentic ingredients, we will provide you with the knowledge and inspiration to embark on your own brewing adventure. Whether you are a seasoned homebrewer or a craft beer enthusiast, this subchapter will open up a world of possibilities.

So, grab a pint, sit back, and join us on a journey to revive forgotten beer styles. From forgotten classics to ancient recipes, we will explore the endless possibilities and celebrate the diversity of beer. Cheers to the past, present, and future of brewing!

Incorporating Cultural Influences in Brewing

Beer, as we know it today, has a rich and diverse history that spans across cultures and continents. Each region has its own unique brewing traditions and techniques, resulting in a wide variety of flavors and styles. Incorporating cultural influences in brewing not only adds depth and complexity to your beer but also allows you to explore the world of brewing in a whole new way.

One of the most exciting aspects of brewing is the opportunity to experiment with different ingredients and flavors. By taking inspiration from various cultures, you can create beers that pay homage to traditional brewing methods while adding your own modern twist. For example, you might incorporate spices commonly used in Indian cuisine to create a flavorful and aromatic Indian-inspired IPA. Or perhaps you could infuse your brew with the tropical fruits of the Caribbean, giving it a refreshing and exotic twist.

Craft beer production techniques also play a significant role in incorporating cultural influences. By embracing the art of craft brewing, you can experiment with small-batch production methods that allow for greater creativity and innovation. This opens up endless possibilities for creating unique beers that reflect the flavors and traditions of different cultures.

Home brewing, too, provides a fantastic opportunity to incorporate cultural influences. As a beginner brewer, you can start by exploring recipes from around the world and experimenting with different ingredients and techniques. This not only allows you to develop your brewing skills but also exposes you to a wide range of flavors and styles. Whether you're brewing a classic German lager or a rich and malty Irish stout, each batch offers a chance to dive into the cultural heritage of the beer you're producing.

Incorporating cultural influences in brewing goes beyond just the ingredients and techniques. It's also about understanding and appreciating the history and traditions behind each beer style. By learning about the brewing methods used in different countries, you gain a deeper appreciation for the craft and can better understand how to create authentic and delicious beers.

So, whether you're interested in brewing traditional Belgian lambics, experimenting with gluten-free recipes, or aging your beer in oak barrels, incorporating cultural influences in your brewing will open up a world of possibilities. It allows you to explore new flavors, pay homage to brewing traditions, and create beers that truly reflect your own unique style. Cheers to embracing the cultural diversity of beer and raising a glass to the incredible world of brewing!

Chapter 7: Gluten-Free Beer Production

Understanding Gluten and its Effects

Gluten is a protein found in grains such as wheat, barley, and rye. It is responsible for giving dough its elasticity and helps bread to rise. However, for some individuals, consuming gluten can lead to adverse effects. In this subchapter, we will delve into the topic of gluten and its effects, particularly in the context of beer production and consumption.

For beer drinkers who are sensitive to gluten or have celiac disease, it is crucial to understand the potential risks associated with traditional beer. Traditional beer is typically brewed using malted barley, which contains gluten. As a result, individuals with gluten sensitivities may experience digestive issues, inflammation, and other uncomfortable symptoms when consuming regular beer.

However, the good news is that the craft beer industry has made significant strides in producing gluten-free beer options. Brewers have experimented with various alternative grains such as sorghum, rice, corn, and even quinoa to create flavorful gluten-free beers. These alternatives provide options for individuals with gluten sensitivities to still enjoy a cold, refreshing beer without any adverse effects.

Gluten-free beer production techniques have evolved over time, allowing brewers to create beers that closely mimic the taste and characteristics of traditional beer. By using enzymes to break down the gluten proteins or incorporating gluten-free grains, breweries have successfully produced a wide range of gluten-free styles, including IPAs, stouts, and lagers.

Home brewing enthusiasts can also try their hand at producing gluten-free beer. With the availability of gluten-free malt extracts and gluten-free grains, home brewers can easily create their own delicious gluten-free brews. This opens up a world of possibilities for those who want to experiment with flavors and styles while catering to their dietary needs.

In conclusion, understanding gluten and its effects is vital for beer drinkers, particularly those with gluten sensitivities. The rise of gluten-free beer production techniques and the availability of ingredients have revolutionized the craft beer industry, offering a diverse range of options for individuals who want to enjoy beer without compromising their health. Whether you are a beer drinker with gluten sensitivities or simply curious about the evolving beer market, exploring gluten-free beer production and its possibilities is an exciting endeavor that is sure to enhance your beer-drinking experience.

Gluten-Free Ingredients and Substitutes

For beer enthusiasts with gluten sensitivities or those simply looking for a gluten-free option, brewing your own gluten-free beer can be an exciting and rewarding experience. In this subchapter, we will explore the various gluten-free ingredients and substitutes you can use to produce delicious gluten-free beer right in the comfort of your own home.

One of the key ingredients in traditional beer production is malted barley, which contains gluten. However, there are several gluten-free alternatives that can be used as substitutes. One popular option is using grains such as millet, sorghum, or rice. These grains can be malted to create malted millet, sorghum, or rice, which can then be used in the brewing process. Another option is using gluten-free malt extracts, which are derived from non-gluten grains like corn or rice. These extracts provide a convenient and easy way to add flavor and sweetness to your gluten-free beer.

In addition to grains, you can also incorporate a variety of gluten-free adjuncts and sugars to enhance the flavor and body of your beer. Examples of gluten-free adjuncts include corn, quinoa, buckwheat, and amaranth. These adjuncts not only contribute unique flavors but also help improve the mouthfeel and overall character of your beer. As for sugars, options like honey, maple syrup, or agave nectar can be used to provide fermentable sugars and add complexity to your gluten-free brew.

To ensure that your gluten-free beer is free from any cross-contamination, it is important to use gluten-free yeast strains. These specialized yeast strains are carefully selected to ensure they do not contain any gluten. There are several commercially available gluten-free yeast options suitable for brewing gluten-free beer.

When it comes to brewing gluten-free beer, it is crucial to pay attention to the quality of your ingredients. Always choose certified gluten-free products and ensure that your equipment is thoroughly cleaned and sanitized to avoid any potential cross-contamination.

Brewing your own gluten-free beer allows you to experiment with different flavors and styles, catering to your personal preferences. Whether you prefer a hop-forward IPA or a rich and malty stout, the world of gluten-free brewing offers endless possibilities.

In conclusion, brewing gluten-free beer can be an exciting and fulfilling endeavor. By utilizing gluten-free ingredients and substitutes, you can produce a wide range of delicious gluten-free beers that cater to your individual taste. So, grab your brewing equipment and embark on a gluten-free brewing adventure that will delight both your taste buds and your passion for beer.

Gluten-Free Brewing Techniques

For beer enthusiasts with gluten sensitivities or those seeking a healthier alternative, gluten-free beer production has become an increasingly popular trend in the craft beer industry. This subchapter explores the brewing techniques and ingredients used to create delicious gluten-free beers, ensuring that everyone can enjoy a cold brew without compromising their dietary restrictions.

Traditionally, beer is made from barley, which contains gluten. However, with advancements in brewing techniques, it is now possible to produce gluten-free beers using alternative grains such as rice, corn, sorghum, or millet. These grains serve as excellent substitutes and provide a base for gluten-free brewing.

One of the essential steps in gluten-free brewing is the malt conversion process. Instead of using malted barley, enzymes like amylase are added to convert the starches from the alternative grains into fermentable sugars. This ensures that the yeast has something to feed on during fermentation and produces alcohol.

In addition to alternative grains, brewers often incorporate specialty ingredients to enhance the flavor profile of gluten-free beers. Fruits, herbs, spices, and even hops can be used to add unique and distinct characteristics. These ingredients not only contribute to the overall taste but also help mask any potential off-flavors that can arise from using alternative grains.

Another crucial aspect of gluten-free brewing is maintaining a strict gluten-free environment throughout the brewing process. Cross-contamination can occur, so it is important to thoroughly clean and sanitize all equipment, including fermenters, hoses, and kegs. Brewers may even designate specific equipment solely for gluten-free brewing to avoid any unintended gluten exposure.

Gluten-free beers come in a variety of styles, ranging from light and crisp lagers to hop-forward IPAs and rich stouts. Craft breweries specializing in gluten-free brewing have been pushing the boundaries, experimenting with different ingredients and techniques to produce high-quality gluten-free beers that can rival their gluten-containing counterparts.

Whether you have celiac disease, gluten intolerance, or simply prefer a gluten-free lifestyle, the availability and quality of gluten-free beers have greatly improved. With the right techniques and ingredients, brewers can create delicious gluten-free beers that cater to the diverse tastes and preferences of beer drinkers worldwide. So raise a glass and savor the flavors of the gluten-free brewing revolution!

Popular Gluten-Free Beer Styles

For those who follow a gluten-free diet or have gluten sensitivities, the world of beer can often seem off-limits. However, with the rise in demand for gluten-free products, the beer industry has stepped up to the challenge, producing a variety of gluten-free beer styles that cater to all taste preferences. In this subchapter, we will explore some of the most popular gluten-free beer styles available today.

1. Gluten-Free Pale Ale: This style is known for its hop-forward flavor profile, balanced by a malty backbone. It offers a refreshing and crisp drinking experience, perfect for those who enjoy a lighter beer with a touch of bitterness.

2. Gluten-Free IPA: IPA lovers can rejoice, as gluten-free versions of this beloved style are now widely available. These beers showcase bold hop aromas and flavors, often with a citrusy or piney character, providing a satisfyingly bitter and aromatic experience.

3. Gluten-Free Amber Ale: With its rich amber color and malty sweetness, this style offers a smooth and full-bodied drinking

experience. It often features caramel and toasty flavors, making it a great choice for those who prefer a more robust beer.

4. Gluten-Free Stout: Dark and velvety, gluten-free stouts offer a complex blend of roasted malt flavors, with hints of chocolate and coffee. They provide a full-bodied and creamy mouthfeel, making them an indulgent choice for beer enthusiasts.

5. Gluten-Free Belgian Tripel: This style is known for its strong and complex flavor profile, with fruity esters and spicy phenols. Gluten-free versions of Belgian Tripels often incorporate alternative grains and yeast strains, resulting in a unique and delicious beer.

These popular gluten-free beer styles not only cater to those with gluten sensitivities but also offer a diverse range of flavors for all beer drinkers to enjoy. Whether you prefer a light and hoppy pale ale or a rich and indulgent stout, there is a gluten-free beer style to suit every palate.

As the demand for gluten-free products continues to grow, so does the availability and variety of gluten-free beer styles. Brewers are constantly experimenting with new ingredients and techniques to produce high-quality gluten-free beers that rival their traditional counterparts. So, next time you're craving a cold one, don't let dietary restrictions hold you back – grab a gluten-free beer and savor the flavors of the craft beer world. Cheers!

Gluten-Free Beer Recipes and Variations

For all the beer enthusiasts who follow a gluten-free diet, this subchapter is dedicated to exploring the world of gluten-free beer production. We understand that beer is not just a beverage for you; it's a passion and a way of life. That's why we have curated this collection of gluten-free beer recipes and variations, ensuring that you can enjoy your favorite drink without compromising on taste or quality.

1. Classic Gluten-Free Lager: This recipe will guide you through the process of brewing a crisp and refreshing lager using gluten-free grains such as millet, sorghum, and rice. You'll learn techniques to balance the flavors and achieve the perfect level of carbonation.

2. Hoppy Gluten-Free IPA: If you're a fan of hop-forward beers, this recipe is for you. Discover how to create a gluten-free IPA bursting with aromatic hops, citrusy flavors, and a pleasant bitterness. We'll also discuss alternative gluten-free grains that can bring complexity to your brew.

3. Belgian-style Gluten-Free Ale: Dive into the world of Belgian ales with this gluten-free twist. Learn about the unique yeast strains and spices that give Belgian beers their distinctive flavors. We'll show you how to achieve the characteristic fruity esters and spicy notes even without using traditional malted barley.

4. Wheat-free Hefeweizen: Hefeweizens are renowned for their banana and clove aromas, but we'll show you how to achieve those flavors without using wheat. Discover alternative grains and techniques to produce a gluten-free version of this classic German wheat beer.

5. Experimental Gluten-Free Beers: Break free from the boundaries of traditional beer styles and explore your creativity. We'll introduce you to a range of gluten-free ingredients like quinoa, buckwheat, and amaranth, and guide you through the process of designing your own unique gluten-free beer.

With these recipes and variations, you can now embark on a gluten-free brewing journey and expand your repertoire of beer styles. Whether you're a homebrewer or a craft beer enthusiast, this subchapter will equip you with the knowledge and techniques to produce exceptional gluten-free beers that rival their gluten-containing counterparts.

Remember, brewing gluten-free beer is not just about catering to dietary restrictions; it's about pushing the boundaries of flavor and innovation. So grab your brewing equipment, source the finest gluten-free ingredients, and get ready to create beer that everyone can enjoy. Cheers to gluten-free brewing!

Addressing Cross-Contamination Concerns

When it comes to producing beer, one of the most important considerations is ensuring that your brewing process is free from any cross-contamination. Cross-contamination occurs when unwanted microorganisms or foreign substances are introduced into your beer, potentially affecting its taste, quality, and safety. In this subchapter, we will explore some essential guidelines and best practices to address cross-contamination concerns in your brewing process.

First and foremost, it is crucial to maintain a clean and sanitized brewing environment. This includes regularly cleaning and sanitizing all equipment, utensils, and surfaces used in the brewing process. Use a food-grade sanitizer to eliminate any potential contaminants and ensure that all equipment is thoroughly rinsed to avoid any residue that could impact the flavor of your beer.

Additionally, proper handling of ingredients is essential to prevent cross-contamination. Be vigilant when handling hops, yeast, and other ingredients, as they can carry unwanted microorganisms. Store ingredients in a cool, dry, and clean area, and always inspect them for any signs of spoilage or contamination before use.

Another crucial step in addressing cross-contamination concerns is to practice good personal hygiene. Always wash your hands thoroughly before handling any brewing equipment or ingredients. Avoid touching your face, hair, or other surfaces that could introduce unwanted bacteria or other contaminants into your beer.

Furthermore, consider implementing a dedicated brewing space or separate designated areas for different stages of the brewing process. This will help minimize the risk of cross-contamination by preventing the mixing of ingredients or equipment used at different stages.

Lastly, be mindful of the potential risks associated with allergens, such as gluten. If you are producing gluten-free beer or catering to individuals with gluten sensitivities, ensure that you have separate equipment and a designated area to prevent any cross-contamination with gluten-containing ingredients.

By following these guidelines and best practices, you can significantly reduce the risk of cross-contamination in your brewing process. This will not only help maintain the quality and taste of your beer but also ensure the safety of your final product. Cheers to producing beer that is free from unwanted contaminants!

Chapter 8: Barrel-Aged Beer Production

The Art of Barrel Aging

Barrel aging beer is an age-old technique that adds complexity and depth to the final product. In this subchapter, we will explore the fascinating world of barrel-aged beer production and how it can elevate your brewing game to new heights.

Barrel aging involves storing beer in wooden barrels, typically made of oak, for an extended period of time. During this aging process, the beer interacts with the wood, absorbing flavors and aromas that can't be replicated in any other way. The result is a beer that is rich, nuanced, and often oozing with character.

One of the key factors in barrel aging is the type of barrel used. Oak barrels are the most common choice due to their porous nature, which allows for the gradual exchange of air and flavors between the beer and the wood. Different types of oak, such as French or American, can also impart distinct flavors to the beer.

The aging period can vary depending on the desired flavor profile. Some brewers prefer a shorter aging period of a few months, while others opt for several years to achieve a more pronounced flavor. The longer the beer ages, the more it develops complexity and smoothness.

Another crucial aspect of barrel aging is the selection of the base beer. Not all beer styles are suitable for barrel aging, as some may clash with the flavors extracted from the wood. Generally, beers with higher alcohol content and robust flavors, such as stouts, barleywines, and sour beers, are ideal for barrel aging.

The process of barrel aging requires patience and careful monitoring. Brewers need to regularly sample the beer to ensure it is developing as intended and to prevent any off-flavors or spoilage. It is a delicate balance between time, temperature, and the unique characteristics of each barrel.

Barrel-aged beers have gained immense popularity in recent years due to their complex flavors and the artistry involved in their production. From bourbon barrel-aged stouts to wine barrel-aged saisons, there is a barrel-aged beer for every palate.

Whether you are a seasoned homebrewer or a craft beer enthusiast, exploring the art of barrel aging opens up a whole new world of possibilities. It allows you to experiment with flavors, push the boundaries of traditional brewing, and create truly unique and memorable beers.

In the next chapter, we will delve deeper into the specific techniques and considerations involved in barrel-aged beer production. Get ready to unlock the secrets of this ancient art form and elevate your beer-drinking experience to new heights.

Choosing the Right Barrels

Barrel-aged beer is a beloved style among beer enthusiasts, known for its rich flavors and complex aromas. But when it comes to producing barrel-aged beer, choosing the right barrels is crucial. In this subchapter, we will explore the various types of barrels available and how they can impact the flavor profile of your beer.

Oak barrels are the most commonly used type of barrel for aging beer. They impart a unique character to the beer, with notes of vanilla, caramel, and sometimes even a hint of smokiness. American oak barrels tend to be more intense in flavor, while French oak barrels offer a smoother, more subtle influence. When selecting oak barrels, it's important to consider the level of toasting or charring, as this can affect the intensity of flavors.

Another popular option for barrel-aged beer is wine barrels. These barrels have previously held wine, which can add interesting fruity and vinous characteristics to the beer. Red wine barrels are often used for bold, dark beers like stouts and barleywines, while white wine barrels are better suited for lighter styles such as saisons or Belgian ales.

For those looking to experiment, whiskey or bourbon barrels can bring a whole new dimension to your beer. These barrels infuse the beer with the flavors of the spirits, such as vanilla, caramel, and oak. However, it's important to note that the strong flavors of whiskey or bourbon can easily overpower the beer, so it's best to use these barrels with caution and in moderation.

Beyond traditional wood barrels, there are also alternative options available. Stainless steel barrels can be used for aging beer, offering a neutral vessel that allows the flavors of the beer to shine through. Additionally, there are specialty barrels like tequila barrels or rum barrels that can create unique flavor profiles.

When selecting barrels, it's important to consider the size and age of the barrel as well. Smaller barrels will impart flavors more quickly, while larger barrels allow for a longer aging process and more complex flavors. Furthermore, older barrels tend to have milder flavors compared to newer ones, as the wood has been used multiple times and the flavors have mellowed.

In conclusion, choosing the right barrels is a crucial step in producing high-quality barrel-aged beer. Oak, wine, whiskey, and alternative barrels each offer their own distinct flavors, allowing you to create a wide range of unique beer styles. By considering the type, size, age, and previous contents of the barrel, you can craft a barrel-aged beer that is truly exceptional and a delight for beer drinkers to savor.

Wood Characteristics and Flavor Infusion

One of the most crucial factors in producing different kinds of beer is the choice of wood and its inherent characteristics. Wood plays a significant role in flavor infusion and can add depth and complexity to your brews. In this subchapter, we will explore the various wood characteristics and how they can impact your beer.

When it comes to wood selection, there are several options to consider, including oak, cherry, maple, and cedar. Each type of wood imparts distinct flavors and aromas to the beer. For example, oak can contribute vanilla, caramel, and toffee notes, while cherry adds a subtle fruity sweetness. Maple provides a rich, smoky flavor, and cedar gives a pleasant woody and earthy taste.

In addition to the type of wood, the age and treatment of the wood also play a role in flavor infusion. Older, seasoned wood tends to mellow the flavors, while freshly cut wood can be more intense. Wood that has been toasted or charred can provide a smoky or roasted character to the beer.

To infuse the desired flavors into your beer, you can use wood chips, cubes, or barrels. Wood chips and cubes are commonly used in home brewing as they are easily accessible and provide a quick infusion of flavor. However, if you have the resources and patience, aging your beer in wooden barrels can produce exceptional results. Barrel aging allows for a slow and gradual flavor extraction, resulting in a more complex and nuanced beer.

It is important to note that wood can also introduce bacteria and wild yeast into your beer, which may lead to unwanted souring or off-flavors. To mitigate this risk, it is crucial to properly clean and sanitize the wood before use.

Experimentation is key when it comes to wood characteristics and flavor infusion. Different types of wood, aging techniques, and beer styles can yield a wide range of results. Don't be afraid to get creative and try new combinations to find the perfect wood flavor profile for your brew.

In conclusion, wood characteristics and flavor infusion are essential aspects of producing different kinds of beer. Understanding the unique qualities of each wood type and how they interact with your beer will enable you to create distinctive brews that will delight your taste buds. So, grab your wood chips or barrels and embark on a flavorful brewing adventure!

Aging Techniques and Timeframes

Aging beer is a crucial step in the brewing process that can greatly enhance the flavor and complexity of the final product. In this subchapter, we will explore different aging techniques and timeframes that can be employed to produce various kinds of beer.

One of the most common aging techniques used in craft beer production is barrel aging. This method involves aging the beer in wooden barrels, typically made of oak, which impart unique flavors and aromas to the brew. The length of time the beer spends in the barrel can vary depending on the desired outcome, with some beers aging for months or even years. Barrel-aged beers are known for their rich, smooth, and often boozy character, making them a favorite among beer enthusiasts.

Another popular aging technique is fruit infusion. This involves adding fresh or dried fruits to the beer during the aging process, allowing the flavors and sugars from the fruit to mingle with the beer. The length of time for fruit-infused beers can vary, but generally, a few weeks to a few months is sufficient to achieve the desired flavor profile. Fruit-infused beers are loved for their vibrant fruit flavors and refreshing qualities, making them a great choice for those looking for a unique and fruity beer experience.

For those interested in brewing sour beers, aging is a crucial step in achieving the desired tartness and complexity. Sour beers are typically aged for several months to several years, allowing the wild yeast and bacteria present in the beer to work their magic and create the distinct sour flavors. Patience is key when aging sour beers, as the flavors develop slowly over time, resulting in a truly unique and complex brew.

While aging can greatly enhance the flavors of beer, it's important to note that not all styles benefit from extended aging. Some beer styles, such as hop-forward IPAs, are best enjoyed fresh to fully appreciate their hop aromas and flavors.

In conclusion, aging techniques and timeframes play a vital role in producing different kinds of beer. Whether it's barrel aging, fruit infusion, or aging for sour beers, each technique offers the opportunity to create unique and complex flavors. Understanding the appropriate aging timeframes for different beer styles is essential to achieve the best possible results. So grab a cold one, experiment with aging techniques, and enjoy the journey of producing exceptional beers at home. Cheers!

Blending and Enhancing Barrel-Aged Beers

Barrel-aged beers have gained immense popularity in recent years, attracting beer enthusiasts and connoisseurs alike. These beers offer depth, complexity, and unique flavors that cannot be replicated using traditional brewing methods. In this subchapter, we will explore the art of blending and enhancing barrel-aged beers, taking your beer-drinking experience to a whole new level.

Blending barrel-aged beers is an intricate process that requires skill and knowledge. Brewmasters carefully select different barrels with varying aging times and flavors to create a harmonious blend. This allows them to balance out the characteristics of each barrel and create a well-rounded beer. Whether you prefer a strong and robust stout or a smooth and fruity ale, blending barrel-aged beers can help you achieve the perfect balance of flavors.

To enhance the flavors of barrel-aged beers, brewers often introduce additional ingredients during the aging process. This can include adding fruits, spices, or even other types of barrel-aged beers. By doing so, they infuse new layers of complexity and create a truly unique drinking experience. For example, adding fresh berries to a bourbon barrel-aged stout can result in a luscious and fruity beer with hints of vanilla and oak.

Homebrewers can also experiment with blending and enhancing barrel-aged beers. If you are new to brewing, start by selecting a base beer that complements the flavors you wish to achieve. Then, consider aging it in different types of barrels, such as bourbon, wine, or rum barrels, to add depth and complexity. Finally, experiment with blending different batches to find the perfect combination of flavors that suits your palate.

When it comes to barrel-aged beers, patience is key. These beers often require extended aging periods, sometimes for several months or even years. But the wait is well worth it when you finally get to taste the rich and complex flavors that develop over time.

So, whether you are a craft beer enthusiast, a homebrewing beginner, or simply someone looking to expand their beer-drinking horizons, blending and enhancing barrel-aged beers is a journey worth embarking on. Get ready to savor the intricate flavors, experience the depth of character, and elevate your beer-drinking experience to new heights. Cheers!

Barrel-Aged Beer Recipes and Pairings

One of the most exciting and unique aspects of the craft beer world is the art of barrel-aging. Barrel-aged beers are known for their complexity, depth of flavor, and smoothness. In this subchapter, we will explore the fascinating world of barrel-aged beer production and provide you with some mouth-watering recipes and pairings to enhance your beer drinking experience.

Barrel-aging involves the process of aging beer in wooden barrels, typically oak, that were previously used to age spirits such as bourbon or wine. This aging process allows the beer to absorb the flavors and aromas present in the barrel, creating a whole new level of complexity. The resulting beer often features notes of vanilla, caramel, oak, and even hints of the spirit that previously occupied the barrel.

To get started with barrel-aged beer production, you will need a suitable barrel and a beer recipe that pairs well with the flavors imparted by the barrel. A popular choice is a robust stout, as it can stand up to the bold flavors from the barrel. Consider adding ingredients such as cocoa nibs, coffee, or vanilla beans to enhance the flavor profile even further.

For those looking to try their hand at barrel-aging at home, it's important to note that the process requires patience. Aging times can vary, but it's common to let the beer rest in the barrel for several months to a year. The longer the aging period, the more pronounced the flavors will become.

Now, let's move on to the exciting part – beer and food pairings! When it comes to barrel-aged beers, the possibilities are endless. The rich, complex flavors of these beers make them a perfect match for a variety of dishes.

For a decadent pairing, try a barrel-aged barleywine with a rich, chocolatey dessert like flourless chocolate cake or a creamy tiramisu.

The caramel and toffee notes in the beer will complement the sweetness of the dessert, creating a delightful harmony of flavors.

If you prefer savory pairings, a barrel-aged sour beer with a charcuterie board is a match made in heaven. The tartness of the beer cuts through the richness of the cured meats and cheeses, creating a refreshing and palate-cleansing experience.

Whether you're a seasoned beer enthusiast or just starting your journey into the world of craft beer, barrel-aged beers offer a unique and unforgettable drinking experience. So, grab a barrel-aged brew, experiment with your own barrel-aging adventures, and savor the incredible flavors that this brewing technique has to offer. Cheers!

Chapter 9: Fruit-Infused Beer Brewing

Adding Fruits to Beer

One of the most exciting aspects of brewing beer is the ability to experiment with different flavors and ingredients. One way to take your brewing skills to the next level is by adding fruits to your beer. This subchapter will explore the art of fruit-infused beer brewing and provide you with the knowledge and techniques to create unique and delicious brews.

Fruit-infused beers have gained immense popularity among beer enthusiasts in recent years. The addition of fruits can enhance the flavor profile of your beer, adding a refreshing and fruity twist. Whether you prefer a citrusy IPA, a tart cherry sour, or a tropical mango wheat beer, the possibilities are endless when it comes to fruit-infused brews.

When selecting fruits for your beer, it is important to choose ripe and high-quality produce. Fresh fruits such as berries, citrus fruits, tropical fruits, and stone fruits can all be used to infuse your beer with distinct flavors. Experiment with different combinations to find the perfect balance that suits your taste preferences.

To infuse fruits into your beer, there are a few different methods you can use. One method is to add the fruits directly to the fermentation vessel during the primary fermentation stage. This allows the flavors to meld with the beer as it ferments, resulting in a more integrated and complex flavor profile. Another method is to create a fruit puree or extract and add it during the secondary fermentation stage. This method allows for greater control over the intensity of the fruit flavors.

It is important to note that adding fruits to your beer can affect the fermentation process. The sugars present in the fruits can be consumed by the yeast, resulting in additional fermentation and potentially higher alcohol content. It is essential to monitor the fermentation process closely and make adjustments as needed to avoid over-carbonation or off-flavors.

When it comes to fruit-infused beer, the possibilities are endless. From light and refreshing summer ales to rich and decadent stouts, adding fruits can elevate your brews to new heights. So, grab your favorite fruits and get ready to embark on a flavor-filled brewing adventure.

In the next chapter, we will delve into the world of low-alcohol and non-alcoholic beer production, providing you with the techniques to brew flavorful and satisfying brews with reduced alcohol content. Stay tuned for more exciting brewing techniques to expand your beer-making repertoire.

Selecting and Preparing Fruits

When it comes to brewing beer, the possibilities are endless. One way to add a unique twist to your brew is by incorporating fruits. Fruits can add a refreshing flavor profile and aroma to your beer, taking it to a whole new level. In this subchapter, we will guide you through the process of selecting and preparing fruits for your beer brewing adventures.

Selecting the right fruits is crucial to achieving the desired taste in your beer. When choosing fruits, it is important to consider their flavor, acidity, and sweetness. Citrus fruits like oranges and lemons can add a zesty and tangy taste, while berries such as raspberries and strawberries can provide a subtle sweetness. Tropical fruits like mangoes and pineapples can give your beer a tropical twist. Experiment with different fruits to find the perfect combination for your brew.

Once you have selected your fruits, it is time to prepare them for brewing. Start by washing the fruits thoroughly to remove any dirt or chemicals. If you are using citrus fruits, zest them to extract the fragrant oils from the skin. For berries, mash them slightly to release their juices. Tropical fruits should be peeled and chopped into small pieces. Remember to remove any seeds or pits from the fruits as they can result in bitterness.

To extract the maximum flavor from the fruits, you can either add them directly to the fermentation vessel or create a fruit puree. To make a puree, blend the fruits until smooth and strain out any solids. This will ensure that only the essence of the fruits is added to your beer.

The timing of adding fruits to the brewing process is crucial. Most fruits are best added during the secondary fermentation stage. This allows the flavors to fully develop without overpowering the beer. However, some fruits, like citrus, can be added during the boil to create a more pronounced flavor.

Remember to always sanitize your equipment and fruits before adding them to your brew. This will prevent any unwanted bacteria or wild yeast from affecting the fermentation process. Additionally, consider the quantity of fruits you are adding to your beer. Start with small amounts and adjust to taste.

Selecting and preparing fruits for your beer brewing adventures can be a fun and rewarding experience. With the right fruits and techniques, you can create unique and delicious beers that will impress even the most discerning beer drinkers. So, don't be afraid to experiment and let your creativity flow. Cheers to fruit-infused beers!

Enhancing Aromas and Flavors

When it comes to enjoying beer, the aroma and flavor are two essential aspects that can make or break the experience. As a beer drinker, you want to savor every sip and indulge in the rich and complex notes that different kinds of beer have to offer. In this subchapter, we will delve into the art of enhancing aromas and flavors, allowing you to take your beer-drinking experience to a whole new level.

Craft beer production techniques play a significant role in creating unique aromas and flavors. Brewers use a variety of ingredients, such as hops, malts, and specialty grains, to infuse their beers with distinct characteristics. Understanding the role of these ingredients and how they contribute to the overall taste profile can help you appreciate the complexities found in different beer styles.

For home brewing beginners, learning the techniques to enhance aromas and flavors can be a game-changer. From selecting the right hops to experimenting with different yeast strains, there are endless possibilities to create your own flavor profiles. We will provide you with practical tips and step-by-step instructions to help you get started on your home brewing journey.

Brewing sour beers has gained popularity in recent years, with its unique tart and acidic flavors delighting beer enthusiasts. We will explore the techniques behind brewing these mouth-puckering delights and offer guidance on how to balance their flavors with other ingredients.

Traditional brewing methods from around the world have been perfected over centuries, resulting in beers that are deeply rooted in their cultural heritage. By understanding these methods, you can gain insight into the traditional flavors and aromas that have captivated beer drinkers for generations.

For those with dietary restrictions, gluten-free beer production offers a solution for enjoying beer without compromising your health. We will delve into the ingredients and techniques used to create gluten-free alternatives that are just as satisfying.

Fruit-infused beer brewing opens up a whole new world of flavors, as different fruits can impart unique aromas and tastes to your brews. We will guide you through the process of selecting and incorporating various fruits into your beer, ensuring a delicious and refreshing result.

As beer drinkers, we appreciate that not every occasion calls for high-alcohol content. Low-alcohol or non-alcoholic beer production techniques allow you to enjoy a flavorful and refreshing beverage without the buzz.

Brewing seasonal or holiday beers can be a festive and exciting endeavor. We will provide you with recipes and inspiration to create beers that capture the spirit of the season, utilizing seasonal ingredients and traditional flavors.

Lastly, we will explore the art of beer pairing and offer a selection of food recipes that complement different beer styles. Whether you're hosting a dinner party or simply enjoying a casual meal, knowing how to pair your beer with the right dish can elevate your dining experience.

Enhancing aromas and flavors is an essential skill for any beer drinker. By understanding the techniques and ingredients used in different kinds of beer production, you can truly appreciate the nuances and complexities that make each brew unique. So grab a pint, dive into this subchapter, and prepare to embark on a flavorful journey through the world of beer. Cheers!

Primary vs. Secondary Fruit Fermentation

Primary vs. Secondary Fruit Fermentation: Enhancing the Flavors of Your Beer

As beer enthusiasts, we are constantly seeking new ways to elevate our brewing skills and create unique flavors that tantalize our taste buds. One technique that has gained popularity in recent years is fruit fermentation - the process of infusing beer with the luscious flavors of various fruits. However, it is important to understand the difference between primary and secondary fruit fermentation to achieve the desired results.

Primary fruit fermentation involves adding fruits directly into the primary fermentation vessel along with the other ingredients. This method is ideal for fruits with high sugar content, such as berries, cherries, and peaches. The sugars in these fruits provide additional fermentable material for the yeast, resulting in a more robust flavor profile. Primary fermentation typically lasts for a week or two before transferring the beer to a secondary vessel.

On the other hand, secondary fruit fermentation involves adding fruits during the secondary fermentation phase, after the primary fermentation is complete. This method is suitable for fruits with delicate flavors, such as citrus fruits, melons, and tropical fruits. By introducing the fruits at this stage, you can preserve their delicate aromas and avoid any potential overpowering of flavors. Secondary fermentation can take anywhere from a few days to a few weeks, depending on the desired intensity of fruit flavor.

Both primary and secondary fruit fermentation offer their own advantages and challenges. Primary fermentation allows for greater integration of fruit flavors, resulting in a beer that is more harmonious and well-rounded. However, it can also lead to a more pronounced and potentially dominant fruit character. Secondary fermentation, on the other hand, allows for greater control over the fruit flavors, enabling brewers to fine-tune the balance between the base beer and the fruit infusion.

Regardless of which method you choose, it is crucial to select high-quality and ripe fruits to achieve the best results. Thoroughly sanitize all equipment and ensure proper handling of the fruits to prevent contamination. Experiment with different fruits, ratios, and fermentation times to discover your preferred fruit-infused beer styles.

In conclusion, primary and secondary fruit fermentation techniques offer beer drinkers a world of possibilities to explore and create unique flavors. Whether you prefer the boldness of primary fermentation or the subtlety of secondary fermentation, both methods can help you produce exceptional fruit-infused beers that will surely impress your taste buds. Cheers to the endless creativity of brewing!

Fruit-Infused Beer Recipes and Techniques

If you're a beer drinker who loves experimenting with different flavors and styles, then fruit-infused beers are a must-try. This subchapter will delve into the exciting world of fruit-infused beer brewing, providing you with recipes and techniques that will take your beer-drinking experience to new heights.

Fruit-infused beers are a perfect blend of fruity sweetness and the refreshing bitterness of beer. The addition of fruits not only adds a vibrant hue to your brew but also imparts unique flavors and aromas that can transform your favorite beer style into something truly extraordinary.

To start your fruit-infused beer brewing journey, you need to know which fruits pair well with different beer styles. For example, citrus fruits like oranges and grapefruits work beautifully with lighter beer styles such as wheat beers or pale ales. On the other hand, berries like raspberries and blackberries can complement darker beer styles like stouts or porters.

Once you've chosen your fruit, the next step is to decide how you want to incorporate it into your beer. You can use fresh fruits, fruit purees, or even fruit extracts to achieve the desired flavor profile. Each method has its own unique advantages, so experimenting with different techniques is highly encouraged.

In this subchapter, you'll find a collection of tried-and-tested fruit-infused beer recipes that cater to a wide range of tastes. From classic combinations like strawberry blonde ale to more exotic blends such as mango-infused IPA, there's something for everyone to enjoy.

Furthermore, we'll provide you with techniques and tips on how to properly handle and prepare the fruits for infusion, ensuring that you achieve the best possible flavor extraction. You'll also learn about fermentation considerations when working with fruit, as the sugars in fruits can affect the final alcohol content of your brew.

Whether you're an experienced homebrewer or just starting out, fruit-infused beers offer endless possibilities for creativity and experimentation. So grab your brewing equipment, pick your favorite fruits, and get ready to embark on a flavorful journey that will delight your taste buds and impress your friends.

Remember, the key to successful fruit-infused beer brewing is to have fun and let your creativity run wild. So why settle for ordinary when you can experience the extraordinary with fruit-infused beers? Cheers to pushing the boundaries of beer brewing and savoring the delicious fruits of your labor!

Balancing Sweetness and Tartness

One of the most important aspects of producing different kinds of beer is finding the perfect balance between sweetness and tartness. These two flavors can greatly enhance the overall taste and experience of a beer, and mastering this balance is a skill that every beer drinker should strive for.

When it comes to crafting beer, there are various techniques and ingredients that can be used to achieve the desired level of sweetness and tartness. For instance, adding different types of malt can contribute to the sweetness in a beer. Malts such as caramel or chocolate can add a rich and sweet flavor profile, while lighter malts like pilsner or pale malt can offer a more subtle sweetness.

On the other hand, tartness can be achieved through the use of certain yeast strains or the addition of fruits or acidic ingredients. For example, Belgian-style beers often use specific yeast strains that produce a slightly tart or sour flavor. Additionally, fruits like raspberries or cherries can be added during fermentation to create a tangy and refreshing taste.

When trying to balance sweetness and tartness, it's important to consider the style of beer you are producing. Some styles, like IPAs or stouts, may lean more towards sweetness, while others, like Berliner Weiss or Gose, are known for their tartness. Understanding the characteristics of each style and experimenting with different ingredients and techniques will help you find the perfect balance for your beer.

It's also worth noting that personal preference plays a significant role in finding the right balance. Some beer drinkers may prefer sweeter beers, while others enjoy the tartness of a sour brew. As you explore the world of brewing, don't be afraid to experiment and adjust the levels of sweetness and tartness to suit your taste.

In conclusion, balancing sweetness and tartness is a crucial skill for any beer drinker interested in producing different kinds of beer. By understanding the various techniques and ingredients available, as well as considering the style of beer you are producing and personal preferences, you can create a brew that perfectly balances these two flavors. So go ahead, grab your brewing equipment, and start creating your own unique and balanced beers!

Chapter 10: Low-Alcohol or Non-Alcoholic Beer Production

Understanding Low-Alcohol and Non-Alcoholic Beer

Low-alcohol and non-alcoholic beers have been gaining popularity among beer enthusiasts in recent years. Whether you're looking to cut back on alcohol consumption, are a designated driver, or simply want to enjoy the taste of beer without the buzz, these alternatives offer a great solution. In this subchapter, we will delve into the world of low-alcohol and non-alcoholic beer, exploring the production methods, flavors, and benefits they offer.

Low-alcohol beer, also known as light beer or session beer, typically contains less than 3% alcohol by volume (ABV). This is achieved through various brewing techniques, such as reducing the amount of malt used or using special yeast strains that produce less alcohol during fermentation. Despite the lower alcohol content, low-alcohol beers can still provide a satisfying and refreshing beverage experience.

Non-alcoholic beer, on the other hand, contains less than 0.5% ABV. These brews undergo a similar brewing process to regular beer, but the alcohol is removed through methods like vacuum distillation or reverse osmosis. The result is a beverage that retains the flavors and aromas of beer while being virtually alcohol-free.

One of the advantages of low-alcohol and non-alcoholic beers is their ability to be enjoyed in social settings without the negative effects of alcohol. They can be a great option for those who want to maintain clarity of mind or for individuals with health conditions that require alcohol abstinence. Additionally, these beers can be a gateway for individuals who are looking to venture into the world of craft beer but are not yet ready for higher alcohol content.

The flavor profiles of low-alcohol and non-alcoholic beers have come a long way in recent years. Gone are the days when they were considered watery or lacking in taste. Breweries now offer a wide range of styles, from hop-forward IPAs to malty stouts, all with reduced or no alcohol. These beers often exhibit complex flavors, balanced bitterness, and refreshing characteristics, making them a viable alternative to their stronger counterparts.

Whether you're a beer enthusiast looking to explore new flavors, a craft beer producer wanting to expand your offerings, or simply someone interested in a healthier beer option, low-alcohol and non-alcoholic beers provide a compelling choice. With their improved taste profiles and growing availability, they are no longer viewed as inferior substitutes but rather as a valuable addition to the world of beer. So, next time you're in the mood for a brew but don't want the alcohol, give these beers a try and discover a whole new world of flavor.

Reducing Alcohol Content in Beer

When it comes to beer, we all have our preferences. Some enjoy the strong buzz that comes with higher alcohol content, while others prefer a lighter, more sessionable brew. If you fall into the latter category, this subchapter is for you. In the following pages, we will explore various techniques and methods to reduce the alcohol content in your beer, allowing you to enjoy more without the worry of getting too intoxicated.

One popular method of reducing alcohol content is through the process of "dilution." This technique involves adding water to your beer during the brewing process to lower the overall alcohol percentage. However, it's important to note that dilution can affect the flavor and body of your beer, so it's crucial to experiment and find the right balance that suits your taste.

Another method to consider is yeast selection. Different strains of yeast have varying levels of alcohol tolerance. By choosing a yeast strain with a lower tolerance, you can control the alcohol content of your beer. However, it's important to note that this may also affect the flavor profile and fermentation characteristics of your brew.

For those looking for a more natural approach to reducing alcohol content, you may consider using ingredients that naturally have a lower sugar content. By using fewer fermentable sugars in your recipe, you can effectively reduce the alcohol content. This method requires careful consideration and experimentation to ensure that the beer maintains its desired flavor and body.

Additionally, some breweries employ a technique called "reverse osmosis" to reduce alcohol content. This process involves filtering the beer through a specialized membrane that removes alcohol molecules, resulting in a lower alcohol percentage. While this method may require specialized equipment, it offers precise control over the alcohol reduction process.

As a beer drinker, it's important to have options that cater to your preferences. Whether you're looking for a lighter beer to enjoy during long sessions or want to reduce the alcohol content for health or personal reasons, there are numerous methods available to achieve your desired result. Experiment, explore, and most importantly, enjoy the process of producing and consuming your own low-alcohol brews. Cheers to your brewing adventures!

Techniques for Brewing Low-Alcohol Beers

As beer drinkers become more health-conscious and seek lower alcohol options, the demand for low-alcohol or non-alcoholic beers has been on the rise. Brewing low-alcohol beers requires special techniques to ensure the same great taste and quality while reducing the alcohol content. In this subchapter, we will explore some techniques to help you produce delicious low-alcohol beers at home or in your craft brewery.

1. Extended Mashing: One of the key techniques for brewing low-alcohol beers is to extend the mashing process. By increasing the mash time, the enzymes have more time to convert the starches into fermentable sugars, resulting in a higher attenuation and lower alcohol content.

2. Grain Selection: Choosing the right grains is essential for brewing low-alcohol beers. Opt for a high percentage of base malts, such as Pilsner or Pale malt, as they have a lower sugar content and will produce a lighter-bodied beer with less alcohol.

3. Dilution: Another technique is to dilute the wort before fermentation. Adding water to the wort reduces the overall sugar concentration, resulting in a lower alcohol content. However, it's crucial to maintain the desired flavor profile and balance by adjusting the hops and malt accordingly.

4. Yeast Selection: Selecting the appropriate yeast strain is vital for low-alcohol beer production. Choose a yeast with high attenuation, meaning it can ferment a larger portion of the sugars, resulting in a drier and less alcoholic beer.

5. Temperature Control: Proper temperature control during fermentation is crucial for low-alcohol beer production. Lower fermentation temperatures can help reduce the production of higher alcohols and esters, resulting in a cleaner and smoother beer.

6. Hop Utilization: Adjusting the hop additions can help balance the flavors in low-alcohol beers. Increasing the hop bitterness can compensate for the reduced malt sweetness, creating a well-rounded beer with a lower alcohol content.

7. Carbonation: When carbonating low-alcohol beers, it's essential to use the appropriate method. Lower alcohol levels can affect carbonation, so consider using forced carbonation methods like kegging or counter-pressure filling to achieve consistent carbonation levels.

8. Flavor Enhancements: Adding flavor enhancers like fruits, spices, or herbs can help compensate for the lower alcohol content by providing additional complexity and depth of flavor to the beer.

By employing these techniques, you can produce low-alcohol beers that are enjoyable and satisfying for those looking for a lighter drinking experience. Whether you are a homebrewer or a craft beer enthusiast, experimenting with low-alcohol beer production can open up new possibilities and cater to a broader audience of beer drinkers. Cheers to brewing great-tasting, low-alcohol beers!

Non-Alcoholic Fermentation Methods

In the world of beer, the focus is often on the rich flavors and intoxicating effects of alcohol. However, there is a growing demand for non-alcoholic beers that can be enjoyed by those who either choose not to drink alcohol or simply want a refreshing beverage without the buzz. This subchapter will delve into the fascinating world of non-alcoholic fermentation methods, exploring the techniques used to create beer-like beverages with little to no alcohol content.

One of the most common methods for producing non-alcoholic beer is called vacuum distillation. This process involves removing the alcohol from a fully fermented beer through a specialized distillation system that operates under vacuum conditions. By lowering the boiling point of alcohol, it can be separated from the beer, leaving behind the desired flavors and aromas without the alcoholic content.

Another popular technique is known as reverse osmosis. This method involves forcing the beer through a semi-permeable membrane that selectively removes alcohol molecules while retaining the other components of the beer. The resulting liquid can then be blended with unfermented beer to achieve the desired flavor profile.

In recent years, advancements in brewing technology have also led to the development of non-alcoholic beers using yeast strains that produce very little alcohol. These specialized yeast strains are able to consume sugars and produce flavors and aromas similar to traditional beer, but with significantly lower alcohol content.

Non-alcoholic fermentation methods also extend beyond traditional beer styles. Craft brewers have been experimenting with non-alcoholic versions of popular beer styles such as IPAs, stouts, and sours. These beers often utilize techniques like dry hopping, kettle souring, and barrel aging to create complex and flavorful non-alcoholic options.

For those interested in home brewing, there are also methods available to produce non-alcoholic beers in smaller quantities. These techniques often involve using specialized yeast strains, controlling fermentation conditions, and utilizing alternative ingredients such as malt extracts or non-fermentable sugars.

Whether you choose to abstain from alcohol or simply want to enjoy a refreshing beer without the buzz, non-alcoholic fermentation methods provide a wide range of options. From traditional beer styles to innovative craft brews, there is a non-alcoholic beer out there to suit every palate. So raise a glass and toast to the exciting world of non-alcoholic fermentation! Cheers!

Flavorful and Refreshing Non-Alcoholic Beer Styles

For beer enthusiasts who enjoy the taste and experience of beer without the alcohol content, non-alcoholic beer styles offer a flavorful and refreshing alternative. Whether you're a designated driver, a health-conscious individual, or simply prefer a non-alcoholic option, there is a wide range of delicious non-alcoholic beers to explore.

One popular style of non-alcoholic beer is the malt beverage. These beers are brewed using the same ingredients as traditional beers, including malted grains, hops, and yeast. The main difference is that the alcohol is removed through a process called vacuum distillation or reverse osmosis. This method preserves the rich flavors and aromas, resulting in a full-bodied and satisfying non-alcoholic beer.

Another style gaining popularity is the hop-forward non-alcoholic beer. Craft breweries have embraced the challenge of creating hoppy, aromatic beers with zero or low alcohol content. By using a combination of hops known for their citrusy, piney, or floral characteristics, these beers deliver a refreshing burst of hop flavor without the alcohol kick.

Fruit-infused non-alcoholic beers are perfect for those seeking a sweeter, more refreshing option. Brewers experiment with different fruits such as berries, citrus, and tropical fruits to create a delightful blend of flavors. These beers are often light and effervescent, making them a great choice for a hot summer day or a fruity pairing with your favorite dessert.

For those interested in exploring traditional brewing methods from around the world, non-alcoholic beer styles such as the German "weissbier" or Belgian "witbier" offer a unique and authentic experience. These beers are typically brewed with wheat, resulting in a hazy appearance and a clove-like or banana-like flavor profile. The non-alcoholic versions retain these characteristics while providing a low-alcohol or alcohol-free option.

Whether you're a homebrewer looking to experiment with non-alcoholic beer production or a beer drinker seeking new and exciting flavors, exploring the world of non-alcoholic beer styles can be a rewarding experience. With a wide range of options available, from malt beverages to hop-forward brews and fruit-infused delights, there is something for everyone's taste preferences.

So, next time you're craving a flavorful and refreshing beer but want to skip the alcohol, don't hesitate to try one of these non-alcoholic beer styles. You might be pleasantly surprised by the depth of flavor and the satisfying experience they offer. Cheers to enjoying great beer, even without the alcohol!

Tips for Enjoying Low-Alcohol Beers

Low-alcohol beers have gained popularity among beer drinkers in recent years for various reasons. Whether you are looking to cut back on your alcohol intake, maintain a clear mind, or simply enjoy the flavors of beer without the buzz, low-alcohol beers offer a great alternative. Here are some tips to help you fully enjoy the experience of drinking low-alcohol beers:

1. Explore Different Styles: Low-alcohol beers come in a wide range of styles, from light lagers to hoppy IPAs and fruity wheat beers. Experiment with different styles to find the ones that suit your taste buds. Don't be afraid to step out of your comfort zone and try something new.

2. Pay Attention to ABV: Alcohol by volume (ABV) indicates the percentage of alcohol in a beer. Low-alcohol beers typically have an ABV of 0.5% to 3.0%. Pay attention to the ABV when selecting a low-alcohol beer, as it can vary greatly and affect the overall taste and experience.

3. Focus on Flavor: Just because a beer is low in alcohol doesn't mean it lacks flavor. Many breweries have mastered the art of crafting low-alcohol beers that are packed with complex flavors. Look for beers that offer a balance of malts, hops, and other ingredients to ensure an enjoyable drinking experience.

4. Consider the Occasion: Low-alcohol beers are perfect for various occasions, from casual gatherings to afternoon sessions at the pub. They provide a refreshing option that allows you to enjoy the social aspect of beer drinking without the effects of excessive alcohol.

5. Pair with Food: Low-alcohol beers can be excellent companions to a wide range of foods. Experiment with food pairings to enhance the flavors of both the beer and the dish. From light salads to spicy dishes and even desserts, there is a low-alcohol beer to complement every meal.

6. Serve at the Right Temperature: Like any other beer, low-alcohol beers should be served at the appropriate temperature to maximize their flavors. Follow the recommended serving temperature for each style to ensure a satisfying drinking experience.

7. Experiment with Home Brewing: If you enjoy the process of brewing your own beer, consider trying your hand at brewing low-alcohol beers. With the right techniques and ingredients, you can create your own flavorful low-alcohol brews that cater to your personal taste preferences.

Remember, the key to fully enjoying low-alcohol beers is to approach them with an open mind and an appreciation for the craftsmanship that goes into producing these unique brews. So, next time you're looking for a beer that allows you to savor the flavors without the alcohol content, reach for a low-alcohol option and embark on a delightful tasting experience.

Chapter 11: Brewing Seasonal or Holiday Beers

Exploring Seasonal Beer Traditions

As beer enthusiasts, we all appreciate the diverse range of flavors and aromas that different brews offer. But have you ever wondered about the rich history and traditions behind seasonal beer? In this subchapter, we will delve into the fascinating world of seasonal beer traditions and explore how they have shaped the brewing landscape.

Seasonal beers have been brewed for centuries, with each season bringing its own unique ingredients and brewing techniques. From the rich and warming winter ales to the light and refreshing summer brews, seasonal beers offer a delightful array of flavors that perfectly match the changing seasons.

Winter beers are typically characterized by their robust malt profiles, warming spices, and higher alcohol content. These brews are perfect for sipping by the fire on a cold winter's night. In contrast, summer beers are crisp, light, and often infused with fruity flavors, making them the ideal thirst quenchers on hot summer days.

One of the most famous seasonal beer traditions is Oktoberfest, a German festival that celebrates the arrival of autumn. During this time, breweries produce Märzen, a malty and slightly hoppy lager that pairs perfectly with traditional Bavarian cuisine. Oktoberfest has become a global phenomenon, with beer lovers around the world eagerly awaiting the release of these special brews.

But seasonal beer traditions are not limited to Germany. In Belgium, brewers create exquisite Christmas beers, often aged in oak barrels and infused with spices, dried fruits, and even chocolate. These complex and indulgent brews are a true delight for the senses and are best enjoyed during the holiday season.

As craft beer enthusiasts, we can also embrace the art of brewing seasonal beers at home. By experimenting with different ingredients and techniques, we can create our own unique interpretations of these timeless traditions. From brewing a pumpkin ale for Halloween to crafting a floral and citrusy spring beer, the possibilities are endless.

In this subchapter, we will explore the various ingredients, brewing methods, and recipes that are commonly used in seasonal beer production. Whether you are a seasoned homebrewer or just starting out, this guide will provide you with the knowledge and inspiration to create your own seasonal masterpieces.

So grab a pint, sit back, and join us as we embark on a journey through the captivating world of seasonal beer traditions. Cheers to the flavors of the seasons!

Ingredients and Flavors for Seasonal Beers

When it comes to brewing seasonal beers, the possibilities are endless. Each season brings with it a unique set of flavors and ingredients that can be used to create truly remarkable brews. In this subchapter, we will explore the various ingredients and flavors that are commonly used in seasonal beers, providing you with the knowledge you need to produce your own delicious and festive brews.

One of the key aspects of brewing seasonal beers is selecting the right ingredients. Many brewers choose to incorporate seasonal fruits, herbs, and spices into their recipes to capture the essence of the season. For example, in the fall, you might opt for ingredients such as pumpkin, cinnamon, nutmeg, and cloves to create a warm and comforting brew. In the winter, flavors like chocolate, vanilla, and peppermint can add a touch of holiday cheer to your beer. Spring and summer offer a plethora of options, such as citrus fruits, berries, and floral notes, to create refreshing and vibrant brews.

It's important to note that the quality of the ingredients you use will greatly impact the final outcome of your beer. Fresh, locally sourced produce will often yield the best results, so be sure to visit your local farmers' market or specialty store to find the best ingredients for your seasonal brews.

In addition to selecting the right ingredients, it's also crucial to consider the balance of flavors in your seasonal beers. Experimentation is key here, as you'll want to find the right combination of ingredients that complement each other without overpowering the beer. For example, if you're brewing a summer beer with citrus flavors, you'll want to ensure that the tartness of the fruit doesn't overwhelm the overall taste of the beer.

When brewing seasonal beers, it's also worth considering the use of specialty malts and hops that can enhance the desired flavors. For example, using caramel or chocolate malts can add depth and sweetness to fall and winter brews, while using floral or fruity hops can bring out the vibrant flavors of spring and summer ingredients.

By understanding the various ingredients and flavors that are commonly used in seasonal beers, you'll be well-equipped to create your own unique and delicious brews. Whether you're brewing a spiced pumpkin ale for Halloween or a refreshing citrus-infused beer for a summer barbecue, the possibilities are endless. So grab your brewing equipment and let your creativity flow as you embark on the journey of crafting your very own seasonal beers. Cheers!

Brewing Techniques for Seasonal Varieties

Seasonal beers are a delightful treat for beer enthusiasts as they capture the essence and flavors of specific times of the year. From refreshing summer ales to rich winter stouts, brewing seasonal varieties requires a unique set of techniques to ensure the perfect balance of flavors. In this subchapter, we will explore the brewing techniques for seasonal varieties and how you can create your own array of delicious seasonal brews.

When it comes to brewing seasonal beers, the key is to create a harmonious blend of ingredients that reflect the spirit of the season. For example, for a summer beer, you may want to incorporate light and refreshing ingredients such as citrus fruits or floral hops. On the other hand, for a winter beer, you might opt for darker malts or spices like cinnamon and nutmeg to create a cozy and warming brew.

One important aspect of brewing seasonal beers is understanding the timing and temperature control during fermentation. Temperature plays a significant role in the flavor development of your beer. For example, if you are brewing a crisp autumn ale, you might want to ferment at a slightly cooler temperature to enhance the flavors of the hops and create a clean finish. Alternatively, if you are brewing a winter warmer, a warmer fermentation temperature can help bring out the complexities of the malts and spices.

Another technique to consider is the use of specialty grains. Adding specialty grains like caramel or chocolate malts can provide a depth of flavor and complexity to your seasonal brews. These grains can be steeped in hot water before the boiling process, extracting their sugars and flavors, which will be later fermented by the yeast.

Furthermore, experimenting with different yeast strains can play a crucial role in the outcome of your seasonal beers. Certain yeast strains produce unique flavors and aromas that can complement the chosen season. For example, a Belgian yeast strain can contribute fruity and spicy notes to a spring saison, while an English ale yeast can enhance the nutty flavors of an autumn brown ale.

In conclusion, brewing seasonal varieties requires a thoughtful approach to ingredient selection, timing, and temperature control. By understanding the unique characteristics of each season and implementing the appropriate techniques, you can create a diverse range of flavorful and enjoyable brews. So, why not embark on the journey of brewing your very own seasonal beers and elevate your beer-drinking experience throughout the year? Cheers to that!

Spiced and Winter Warmer Styles

When the cold weather hits and the holiday season approaches, there's nothing quite like cozying up with a spiced and winter warmer beer. These styles are designed to bring warmth and comfort during those chilly months, and they often feature a unique blend of spices and flavors that perfectly complement the season.

One popular style within this category is the Winter Ale. These beers are typically full-bodied and malt-forward, with a rich and complex flavor profile. They often feature notes of caramel, toffee, and chocolate, which provide a comforting sweetness. To add a festive touch, brewers often incorporate spices such as cinnamon, nutmeg, and clove, which add a delightful warmth and depth to the beer.

Another beloved style is the Pumpkin Ale. This beer is a staple during the fall season and is often associated with Halloween and Thanksgiving. Pumpkin Ales are brewed using real pumpkin puree and a mixture of spices like cinnamon, ginger, and allspice. The result is a beer that is reminiscent of pumpkin pie, with a creamy texture and a hint of sweetness.

For those looking for a more adventurous flavor experience, there are also beers infused with fruits and spices. These beers often feature bold flavors such as cherry, raspberry, or cranberry, which add a tart and fruity element. Spices like coriander, cardamom, or orange peel can also be added to create a unique and refreshing taste.

Homebrewers can experiment with these styles by adding their own twists. Whether it's using different types of spices, adjusting the level of sweetness, or even incorporating seasonal fruits, the possibilities are endless. The key is to find a balance between the flavors, ensuring that they complement and enhance each other.

When it comes to pairing spiced and winter warmer beers, the options are vast. These styles pair exceptionally well with hearty and rich dishes, such as stews, roasts, or even chocolate desserts. The bold and robust flavors of these beers can stand up to strong and flavorful foods, creating a harmonious and satisfying combination.

In conclusion, spiced and winter warmer styles offer beer drinkers a unique and flavorful experience during the colder months. With their rich malt profiles, festive spices, and sometimes fruity additions, these beers are the perfect accompaniment to cozy nights by the fire or holiday gatherings. So grab a glass, savor the aromas, and enjoy the warmth and comfort that these styles bring. Cheers!

Festive Ale Recipes and Pairings

In this subchapter, we will explore the delightful world of festive ale recipes and pairings, perfect for beer drinkers who enjoy the art of brewing and the joy of celebrating special occasions. Whether you are a homebrewing beginner or a seasoned craft beer enthusiast, these recipes and pairings will surely add a touch of merriment to your beer-drinking experience.

1. Spiced Winter Ale: This recipe combines traditional brewing techniques with festive spices like cinnamon, nutmeg, and cloves. The result is a rich and flavorful ale that warms the soul on cold winter

nights. Pair it with hearty dishes like roasted meats, stews, or gingerbread cookies.

2. Pumpkin Ale: A classic autumn favorite, this recipe infuses the flavors of pumpkin, cinnamon, and ginger into a smooth and creamy ale. Serve it alongside Thanksgiving dinner or enjoy it with pumpkin pie for a truly festive experience.

3. Cherry Stout: This fruity and indulgent stout is a perfect choice for the holiday season. The rich flavors of dark chocolate and tart cherries create a decadent treat that pairs well with chocolate desserts or a cheese platter.

4. Cranberry Wheat Beer: Brewed with fresh cranberries, this light and refreshing wheat beer is a great option for those who prefer a lighter festive brew. Its tangy and fruity notes make it an ideal pairing for Thanksgiving turkey or cranberry sauce.

5. Belgian Christmas Ale: This complex and aromatic ale is brewed with a blend of spices, including coriander, orange peel, and cloves. Its bold flavors and higher alcohol content make it an excellent choice for special celebrations. Pair it with bold cheeses, smoked meats, or spiced nuts.

Remember, brewing these festive ales requires attention to detail and a thorough understanding of craft beer production techniques. Experiment with different ingredients and techniques to create your own unique festive brews. And when it comes to pairing your creations with food, let your imagination run wild. The world of food and beer pairing is vast, and there are no limits to the delicious combinations you can discover.

So, grab your brewing equipment, put on your favorite holiday tunes, and get ready to brew up some festive ale magic. Cheers to the joy of beer brewing and the celebration of special moments with loved ones!

Celebrating Beer Holidays and Festivals

Beer is not just a beverage; it's a way of life for many beer enthusiasts. The world of beer is full of traditions, celebrations, and festivals that bring people together to revel in the joy of brewing and drinking this delightful beverage. In this subchapter, we will explore some of the most popular beer holidays and festivals around the world, where beer drinkers can immerse themselves in the rich culture and history of brewing.

One of the most iconic beer festivals is Oktoberfest, held annually in Munich, Germany. This sixteen-day celebration showcases the best of German brewing traditions, with millions of visitors indulging in traditional Bavarian beer styles such as Märzen and Helles. Attendees can enjoy lively music, delicious food, and the famous beer tents, where they can raise a glass and toast to the spirit of Oktoberfest.

Another notable event is the Great American Beer Festival, held in Denver, Colorado. This festival showcases over 4,000 different beers from more than 800 American breweries. Beer lovers from all over the country gather to sample a wide variety of styles, attend educational seminars, and witness the prestigious beer competition, where breweries strive to win gold, silver, and bronze medals in various categories.

For those interested in exploring unique and experimental brews, the Oregon Brewers Festival in Portland is a must-visit. This festival features over 80 breweries, each offering at least one beer made exclusively for the event. From barrel-aged stouts to fruit-infused ales, attendees can taste a plethora of innovative creations while enjoying the vibrant atmosphere of Portland's waterfront.

Aside from these major festivals, there are numerous beer holidays celebrated throughout the year. Saint Patrick's Day, for example, is synonymous with enjoying a pint of Irish stout like Guinness, while Cinco de Mayo calls for sipping on Mexican-style lagers and cervezas. Christmas and New Year's Eve also have their own beer traditions, with breweries crafting special seasonal releases to spread holiday cheer.

These beer holidays and festivals offer beer drinkers a chance to explore different styles, taste unique brews, and connect with fellow enthusiasts. Whether you're a homebrewer or simply enjoy savoring a well-crafted pint, these celebrations are a testament to the enduring popularity of beer and its ability to bring people together.

In the following chapters, we will delve deeper into the techniques and methods used in producing different kinds of beer, including craft beer production, home brewing for beginners, and traditional brewing methods from around the world. So grab a cold one, and let's embark on a journey through the fascinating world of beer production and appreciation!

Chapter 12: Beer Pairing and Food Recipes

The Basics of Beer and Food Pairing

One of the most enjoyable aspects of being a beer drinker is the opportunity to pair your favorite brews with delicious food. The right combination can elevate both the beer and the dish, creating a memorable dining experience. In this subchapter, we will explore the basics of beer and food pairing, helping you to enhance your beer-drinking journey.

Understanding the basic principles of beer and food pairing is essential. The goal is to find complementary flavors, rather than overpowering or clashing ones. The first step is to consider the characteristics of the beer you are drinking. Is it light or dark? Bitter or sweet? Hoppy or malty? These attributes will guide you in selecting food that will harmonize with the beer's flavors.

Light beers, such as pilsners or lagers, pair well with delicate dishes like seafood, salads, or light cheeses. Their crisp and refreshing nature balances the flavors and cleanses the palate. On the other hand, dark and malty beers like stouts or porters go hand in hand with hearty dishes like grilled meats, chocolate desserts, or smoked cheeses. The rich flavors of these beers complement the richness of the food.

When it comes to hoppy beers like IPAs, their bitterness can be balanced with spicy or salty foods. Indian cuisine, for example, often pairs wonderfully with hoppy beers due to the use of spices. Additionally, the carbonation in beer can help cut through the richness of fatty foods, making them an excellent choice for burgers, fried dishes, or cheese plates.

Another important factor to consider is the regional cuisine. Traditional brewing methods from around the world have shaped the local food culture, resulting in natural beer and food pairings. For example, Belgian beers like saisons or tripels are often enjoyed with mussels or Belgian waffles, while German beers like wheat beers pair well with bratwurst or pretzels.

In this subchapter, we will provide you with a variety of beer and food pairing suggestions. From classic combinations to innovative pairings, you will discover new and exciting ways to elevate your beer-drinking experience. Whether you are hosting a dinner party or simply enjoying a beer and snack at home, understanding the basics of beer and food pairing will undoubtedly enhance your enjoyment of both. Cheers to finding the perfect match!

Complementary and Contrasting Flavors

When it comes to brewing beer, one of the most important aspects to consider is the flavor profile. Creating a well-balanced and enjoyable beer involves understanding how different flavors work together and how they can either complement or contrast each other. In this subchapter, we will dive into the fascinating world of complementary and contrasting flavors in beer production.

Complementary flavors are those that enhance and bring out the best in each other. They create a harmonious balance that results in a more well-rounded and satisfying drinking experience. For example, the rich and malty flavors of a stout can be complemented by the bitterness and citrusy notes of hops. This combination creates a perfect balance between sweetness and bitterness, making the beer more enjoyable to drink.

On the other hand, contrasting flavors can add an exciting and unexpected twist to a beer. By combining flavors that are seemingly opposite, brewers can create unique and memorable taste experiences. For instance, pairing a tart and fruity flavor, like raspberry, with a rich and chocolatey stout can create a delightful contrast that surprises the palate.

Craft beer production techniques allow brewers to experiment with a wide range of flavors and ingredients. From fruit-infused beers to barrel-aged creations, the possibilities are endless. By understanding the principles of complementary and contrasting flavors, brewers can push the boundaries of traditional brewing and create innovative and exciting new beer styles.

Home brewing for beginners is a great way to start exploring the world of complementary and contrasting flavors. As you gain experience and confidence, you can experiment with different ingredients and techniques to create your own unique flavor profiles. Whether you're brewing a classic style or a bold and experimental beer, understanding how flavors interact will help you create exceptional brews that stand out from the crowd.

For those interested in gluten-free beer production, fruit-infused beer brewing, or low-alcohol/non-alcoholic beer production, understanding complementary and contrasting flavors becomes even more critical. These specialty beers often require additional creativity and ingenuity to achieve a well-balanced and satisfying taste.

In conclusion, understanding complementary and contrasting flavors is essential for producing different kinds of beer. Whether you're a homebrewer or a craft beer enthusiast, knowing how flavors work together will allow you to create exceptional brews that excite the palate. So, go ahead and experiment with different flavor combinations, and let your creativity run wild in the pursuit of the perfect pint!

Pairing Beer with Different Cuisines

One of the most enjoyable aspects of being a beer drinker is exploring the endless possibilities of pairing beer with different cuisines. Just like wine, beer has the ability to enhance the flavors of food and create a harmonious dining experience. In this subchapter, we will explore some classic and unconventional beer and cuisine pairings that are sure to elevate your taste buds.

When it comes to pairing beer with different cuisines, it's essential to consider the flavors, textures, and spices of the dish. For example, a light and refreshing pilsner or lager goes perfectly with spicy Mexican dishes such as tacos or enchiladas. The crispness of the beer helps to cleanse the palate and balance out the heat.

If you're indulging in Italian cuisine, reach for a beer with malty and hoppy characteristics like an amber ale or a pale ale. These beers complement the rich tomato-based sauces and the cheesy goodness of pizza and pasta dishes.

For those who enjoy Asian cuisine, the possibilities are endless. Light and delicate dishes like sushi or sashimi pair well with a clean and crisp lager or a light wheat beer. If you're craving something more robust like a stir-fry or a curry, opt for a hoppy IPA or a malty brown ale to stand up to the bold flavors.

When it comes to pairing beer with desserts, don't shy away from experimentation. A rich and chocolaty stout or porter is the perfect match for desserts like chocolate cake or brownies. The roasted flavors in the beer complement the sweetness of the dessert, creating a decadent combination.

For those looking to take their beer and cuisine pairings to the next level, consider exploring the world of craft beers. Craft breweries are known for pushing boundaries and experimenting with unique flavors.

Look for beers infused with fruits, spices, or aged in barrels for a truly extraordinary pairing experience.

In conclusion, pairing beer with different cuisines is a delightful adventure that allows you to explore the endless possibilities of flavor combinations. Whether you're enjoying a traditional dish or experimenting with fusion cuisine, there is a beer out there that will enhance your dining experience. So, grab a cold one and embark on a culinary journey like no other. Cheers!

Cooking with Beer: Recipes and Techniques

Beer is not just for drinking – it can also add incredible flavor and depth to your favorite dishes. In this subchapter, we will explore the world of cooking with beer, providing you with delicious recipes and techniques that will take your culinary skills to new heights.

1. Beer-Marinated Meats: Discover the art of marinating meats with different beer styles to infuse them with unique flavors. From tenderizing steaks with a stout to adding a citrusy twist to chicken with a wheat beer, we will guide you through the process step by step.

2. Beer-Battered Delights: Learn how to create the perfect beer batter that will make your fried foods extra crispy and flavorful. Whether you want to make beer-battered fish and chips or beer-battered onion rings, we have got you covered.

3. Beer-infused Sauces and Gravies: Elevate your sauces and gravies by incorporating beer into the recipe. From a rich beer-based BBQ sauce to a creamy beer cheese sauce, these recipes will bring a new dimension of taste to your dishes.

4. Beer Bread and Pizza Dough: Discover how to incorporate beer into bread and pizza dough recipes to add a unique flavor profile. From

hearty beer bread to crispy beer-infused pizza crust, we will show you how to achieve that perfect balance of beer and dough.

5. Beer Cocktails and Desserts: Unleash your creativity by exploring the world of beer cocktails and desserts. From refreshing beer mojitos to decadent chocolate stout cake, we will provide you with innovative recipes that will impress your guests.

In addition to the recipes, we will also share techniques and tips on selecting the right beer for cooking, understanding flavor profiles, and how to pair different beer styles with specific dishes. We will also address common questions and concerns related to cooking with beer, such as alcohol content and cooking times.

Whether you are a seasoned beer drinker or a homebrewing enthusiast, this subchapter will take your love for beer to the next level. Get ready to experiment, have fun, and create incredible dishes that showcase the versatility of beer as an ingredient. Cheers to cooking with beer!

Hosting Beer Tasting and Pairing Events

Beer tasting and pairing events are a fantastic way to explore the complex flavors and aromas of different beers while also discovering the perfect food pairings. Whether you're a beer enthusiast looking to expand your knowledge or a casual drinker wanting to have a fun and unique experience, hosting your own beer tasting and pairing event can be a rewarding endeavor. In this subchapter, we will guide you through the process of organizing and hosting successful beer tasting and pairing events.

Firstly, it's important to select a variety of beers that showcase different styles, flavors, and origins. Consider including craft beers, traditional brews from around the world, gluten-free options, barrel-aged beers, fruit-infused brews, and even low-alcohol or non-alcoholic beers to cater to various tastes and preferences. This will ensure that there is something for everyone to enjoy.

Next, create a tasting menu that highlights the unique characteristics of each beer. Provide a brief description of each beer, including its style, brewing techniques, and any interesting facts. Encourage guests to savor the aroma, appearance, and taste of each beer before moving on to the next one. This will create an engaging and interactive experience for everyone involved.

To enhance the tasting experience, consider incorporating food pairings that complement the flavors of the beers. Experiment with different combinations and offer suggestions to your guests. For example, hoppy beers pair well with spicy foods, while malty beers are a great match for rich desserts. Additionally, consider including recipes that incorporate beer as an ingredient, such as beer-battered fish or beer-infused sauces.

When hosting the event, create a relaxed and welcoming atmosphere. Provide tasting sheets for guests to take notes on their favorite beers and pairings. Encourage open discussions and allow guests to share their thoughts and opinions on each beer. This will foster a sense of community and create a memorable experience for everyone involved.

In conclusion, hosting beer tasting and pairing events is a fantastic way to explore the diverse world of beer. By selecting a variety of beers, creating a tasting menu, and incorporating food pairings, you can create an engaging and enjoyable experience for all beer enthusiasts. So gather your friends, grab some beers, and embark on a journey of flavors and aromas that will leave you with a newfound appreciation for the art of beer production and pairing. Cheers!

Beer Cocktails and Mixology

Beer cocktails have gained popularity in recent years as people are seeking new and exciting ways to enjoy their favorite brews. This subchapter explores the world of beer mixology, offering a variety of creative and refreshing recipes that will delight even the most discerning beer drinkers.

One of the most popular beer cocktails is the classic Michelada. This Mexican-inspired drink combines beer with lime juice, hot sauce, Worcestershire sauce, and a variety of spices. The result is a tangy and savory beverage that is perfect for a hot summer day or a spicy meal.

For those looking for a sweeter option, the Shandy is a fantastic choice. This blend of beer and lemonade is light, refreshing, and incredibly easy to make. With just a few ingredients, you can create a delightful beverage that is perfect for picnics or backyard barbecues.

If you're feeling adventurous, why not try a beer-based margarita? This unique twist on a classic cocktail combines beer with tequila, lime juice, and a touch of agave syrup. The result is a tart and bubbly drink that will transport you to a sunny beach in no time.

For beer enthusiasts who enjoy the rich flavors of stout or porter, the Black Velvet is a must-try. This elegant cocktail combines equal parts stout beer and sparkling wine, creating a luxurious and decadent drink that is perfect for special occasions or celebrations.

In addition to these classic beer cocktails, this subchapter also explores the world of beer mixology, offering tips and techniques for creating your own unique concoctions. Whether you're experimenting with different flavors, adding fruits or herbs to your beer, or creating themed cocktails for special events, the possibilities are endless.

From fruity beer punches to spicy beer margaritas, this subchapter has something for every beer drinker's taste. So, grab your favorite brew and get ready to explore the exciting world of beer cocktails and mixology. Cheers!

www.ingramcontent.com/pod-product-compliance
Lightning Source LLC
Chambersburg PA
CBHW022024150726
47990CB00002B/803